CLOSING THE ACHIEVEMENT GAP

How to Reach Limited-Formal-Schooling and Long-Term English Learners

Yvonne S. Freeman

David E. Freeman

with Sandra Mercuri

HEINEMANN
PORTSMOUTH, NH

Heinemann
A division of Reed Elsevier Inc.
361 Hanover Street
Portsmouth, NH 03801–3912
www.heinemann.com

Offices and agents throughout the world

Library of Congress Cataloging-in-Publication Data
Freeman, Yvonne S.
    Closing the achievement gap : how to reach limited-formal-schooling and long-term English learners / Yvonne S. Freeman and David E. Freeman with Sandra Mercuri.
       p. cm.
    Includes bibliographical references and index.
    ISBN 0-325-00273-8 (pbk. : alk. paper)
    1. English language—Study and teaching—Foreign speakers.   2. English language—Study and teaching—United States.   3. English language—Adult education.   I. Freeman, David E.   II. Mercuri, Sandra.   III. Title.

PE1128.A2 F744 2002
428'.0071—dc21   2001007439

Editor: Lois Bridges
Production: Vicki Kasabian
Cover design: Jenny Jensen Greenleaf
Typesetter: PD&PS
Manufacturing: Steve Bernier

Printed in the United States of America on acid-free paper
06 05 04 03 02   VP   2 3 4 5

We dedicate this book to all teachers working with older limited-formal-schooling and long-term English learners, especially Sandra Mercuri, Oscar Hernández, and Grace Klassen, and our daughter, Mary Soto.

Contents

Acknowledgments

Since we began our university teaching careers fifteen years ago, it has been clear to us that it is the public school classroom teachers with whom we work who teach us what is most important about schooling. We owe our greatest debts in the creation of this book to three teachers who have had success with older struggling learners: Sandra Mercuri, Oscar Hernández, and Grace Klassen. Within these pages, readers will learn from their stories and get to know their students. Sandra Mercuri was a graduate student of ours, and has become a colleague and friend. This outstanding educator has been integral to both the conception and the completion of this book. Oscar Hernández was one of Yvonne's first mentees at Fresno Pacific University. Watching his growth as a professional has been exciting. He is now not only a high school classroom teacher, but also a teacher of teachers himself. Grace Klassen has dedicated her life to adolescents, responding to their special needs in a way that is gentle, caring, and inspiring. Working with her has reminded us of the breadth and depth of understanding that an experienced and knowledgeable educator can bring to teaching.

We also wish to thank other teachers who have helped make this book possible. Mary Soto, Sandy Wheeler, Linda Medel, and Lonna Deeter have shared with us their experiences teaching older English learners. In addition, Linda Medel and Veronica Manzo have helped us with research on the Internet and in the library.

Two special teacher educators who need to be acknowledged are Bobbi Jentes Mason and Pam Smith. Bobbi has dedicated her professional career to helping older students develop literacy through a curriculum called The Learning Edge, which she developed. Pam, her colleague, has successfully taught adolescents and is now mentoring those, like Oscar, who teach reading and writing to adolescents.

Our colleagues and the staff at Fresno Pacific University continue to support us through encouragement and by helping us do our work. In particular, we would like to thank Henrietta Siemens, Irma Montemayor, Jean Fennacy, Denette Zaninovich, and Linda Hoff.

The professional staff at Heinemann encourages us to keep writing. They support us through their work on our manuscripts, as well as through consistent positive reinforcement. In particular, we would like to thank our production editor, Vicki Kasabian, who, along with Abby Heim, has creatively and enthusiastically organized the details of turning this manuscript into a book. Maura Sullivan consulted with us and others about the important details of promoting this book and getting it into the hands of teachers who might find it useful.

And finally, we would like to thank our editor, Lois Bridges. Lois is truly an amazing editor and an amazing person. She responded to our every query, every idea, and every written page promptly, thoughtfully, and professionally. But there is more to Lois than her professionalism: She is a wonderfully warm and supportive human being. We appreciate her immensely and are grateful that she is willing to be our editor.

Introduction

English learners come to the United States from all over the world. Many large school districts across the country have more than one hundred different home languages. A recent report (Seufert 1998) shows that since 1995 larger numbers of refugees have arrived in the United States from Africa, eastern Asia, eastern Europe, and Russia than from Southeast Asia or Latin America. The report projected that in the year 2000 there would be eighteen thousand refugees in the United States from Africa and fifty-five thousand from eastern Europe, eastern Asia, and Russia combined. These high projections compare with eight thousand refugees from Southeast Asia and only three thousand from Latin America.

Many of these refugees have experienced war, persecution, pestilence, and famine. Their living conditions have often made schooling impossible. They hope to find a better life in their new country and have dreams of success for their children. Their dreams are not always realized, though, in part because the children begin school here without having had the educational experiences teachers in this country expect. Many have had little schooling, or none at all.

Twelve-year-old Fadumo, her fourteen-year-old brother, Khalid, and their sixteen-year-old brother, Awile, arrived in Kansas as refugees from the Sudan never having had a chance to attend school in their country because of chaotic conditions caused by ethnic and religious wars, famine, and disease. They do not read or write in their first language. They have not developed the academic concepts that other students their age have. And they speak only a little English. They are trying to adjust to living in a new country and attending school where the instruction is presented in an unfamiliar language.

These students are typical of many recent refugees. They have escaped from countries that are in great social upheaval. Even though their social and economic conditions in the United States are better than they were in their native land, these students often live in poverty. They have not developed literacy in their first language, they have not developed the academic concepts that other students their age have, and their English is very limited. Thus, there is a gap between their current language and academic proficiency and the proficiency that schools expect from students their age.

With this continuing influx of refugees, it is no wonder that wherever we travel across the country, teachers ask us how they can meet the needs of their older students who lack adequate formal schooling. Teachers need to prepare these students to compete with native English speakers and with other English learners who are also new arrivals, but who have a strong academic background in their first language. There isn't much time for students who arrive in middle school or high school to catch up. They are many years behind their classmates, but they may have only four or five years to close the achievement gap before they must meet high school graduation requirements and pass exit exams.

Older students with limited formal schooling pose a great challenge to teachers. However, many middle school and secondary teachers we work with report that the English learners who experience the highest rate of academic failure are those who have lived in the United States all their lives. This second group is often referred to as long-term LEP (limited English proficient) students. We prefer to refer to them as long-term English learners to avoid labels that imply a deficiency. These are students who have been in this country for several years or even since birth. They have been in and out of bilingual and ESL (English as a second language) programs, but they have not developed high levels of literacy in either their first language or in English.

Thirteen-year-old Lorena has attended inner-city schools in a midsize city in California since kindergarten. When she was twelve she was raped by an eighteen year old who lived in her apartment complex. She now has a child, and her very traditional Mexican family is ashamed of her situation and keeps her isolated from extended-family members and friends. She is now attending a continuation school, and despite her years of schooling in the U.S., she is more comfortable speaking Spanish than English. She is reading and writing below grade level, but her perception of her academic work is much higher than the reality.

All of Lorena's schooling has been in the United States. However, she did not have a consistent school program that would allow her to develop academic concepts while learning English. Even though she is below grade level, she thinks she is doing well in school. She needs a great deal of help to improve her reading and writing skills in English. In addition, her social situation makes it difficult for her to focus adequately on school. The chances of her closing the achievement gap and completing her high school requirements seem slim.

Some long-term English learners seem to speak English quite well. Others, like Lorena, have very limited English. Even those with conversational English generally do poorly on tests and written assignments. These students often drop out of school quite early. In our local district, the central valley of California, many long-term English learners drop out of school in the eighth or ninth grade. Even those who do continue to attend school may not go regularly and may have negative attitudes toward school. Such students are not easy to reach, even for the best teachers.

Goals and Organization of This Book

This book is meant for teachers, program directors, resource personnel, and administrators who are attempting to meet the needs of older English learners who come to school with limited-formal-schooling experiences, like the Sudanese refugees we described, or those who are long-term English learners, like Lorena. We discuss these types of students in detail, describing their backgrounds and general characteristics as well as factors that influence them and their school achievement.

Since the key goal of this book is to help educators meet the academic needs of these students, we look in detail at what research tells us works best for these two types of English learners. We make suggestions for teaching them, including specific suggestions about classroom environment and routines, activities and strategies that work, and materials that are accessible and useful for teaching academic content. At the end of each chapter, we suggest some professional extension activities to help readers apply the information in this book to their educational settings.

In Chapter 1 we introduce several students and look at the characteristics that lead us to consider them to be either long-term English learners or older English learners who are newly arrived in this country and who have had limited formal schooling. Our aim is to use these specific students to exemplify the characteristics of the two types of older English learners. We then discuss the sociocultural theory developed by Ogbu, which helps account for differences between the two types of English learners. We present four keys for working effectively with older English learners, and we introduce three teachers from whose classrooms we take many examples of effective teaching of older English learners.

In Chapter 2 we present brief case studies of several students who fit each of the two categories: limited-formal-schooling and long-term English learners. We also distinguish between conversational language and the academic English students need to succeed in school.

Chapter 3 reviews the research on effective practices for working with older English learners. We discuss the importance of using a thematic approach to help students develop the academic language and concepts they need. We also explain the differences between two types of classes for English learners: ELD (English language development) and SDAIE (specially designed academic instruction in English).

Chapter 4 discusses the importance of organizing curriculum around themes. We present several examples of theme studies. In addition, we examine more closely the kinds of concepts students need to develop to succeed in school. Further, we consider how concepts learned in a student's first language transfer to English.

In Chapter 5 we look at how different teachers have organized their daily routines to enhance learning. We also consider some of the strategies these teachers have found to be useful, such as using graphic organizers and including time for free voluntary reading. As we describe these routines and strategies, we show how effective teachers scaffold instruction to provide the support students need to develop academic language.

In the final chapter we focus on the effective strategies one teacher uses with her older English learners during a theme study that connects closely with their lives. We describe elements of her curriculum in detail. We return to the four keys we introduced in Chapter 1 and review how the effective teachers described in this book follow those keys to help close the achievement gap for their older English learners.

Terms to Describe Students

As we have done in our other books, we wish to comment on the terminology we use to refer to the students we write about. It is always difficult to choose a descriptive term for any group because any label we choose may limit the people in that group (Wink 1993). For example, the frequently used label for non–English speakers, LEP (limited English proficient), focuses attention on what students cannot do. All of us have limited (or no) proficiency in a number of languages. To refer to some students as "long-term LEP" is even more limiting.

Similarly, a number of terms have been used to describe newly arrived students with limited formal schooling, including "preliterate," "underschooled," "overage," "low-literacy LEP," and "late emergent readers." Some students have been characterized as "nonresilient." All of these terms have negative connotations. These students have important background experiences outside of school that need to be acknowledged, and they have abilities that need to be drawn upon. Indeed, the successful teachers we describe in this book take a positive attitude toward all their students and draw on their students' strengths.

In the past, we have referred to students who do not speak English as their first language as "second-language learners" or "bilingual learners." We used these terms to make the point that they already have another language, and English is an additional language for them. However, we have become uncomfortable with using these terms since we are aware that many English language learners are, in fact, adding a third, fourth, or even fifth language to their repertoire. Therefore, the terms "bilingual learners" and "second-language learners" might also be seen as limiting.

The term we currently use is "English language learners" or simply "English learners." Even native speakers of English are English language learners in a sense, but students for whom English is not the native language face the specific task of learning English. This term focuses on what these students are trying to do and what they have in common, so it is the term we use most frequently.

In this book we limit our focus to two types of English learners. We do not discuss new arrivals to this country who have had adequate formal schooling. We use the term English learner, then, to designate either "newly arrived with limited formal schooling" (LFS) or "long-term English learners" (LTELs). Where it is helpful to distinguish between those two types of English learners, we do so.

Conclusion

As with the other books we have written, we have relied extensively on examples from different teachers we work with. About the same time that we started getting questions about how to work with older English learners, Yvonne was conducting research in Sandra Mercuri's newcomer class. Sandra teaches a multiage fourth- through sixth-grade class in a small farming community. Almost all her students could be classified as having limited formal schooling. Because of the approach to teaching that Sandra has implemented, many of her students succeed.

Yvonne wanted to share Sandra's story, but we were aware that many other older English learners are not new arrivals to the United States. For that reason, Yvonne contacted two other teachers, Oscar and Grace, whose classes have many long-term English learners as well as some limited-formal-schooling students. These three teachers provided many of the examples for this book and helped us understand how to work successfully with older English learners.

This book is based on the same philosophy of teaching and learning as our other books, but the focus has changed. In *Between Worlds: Access to Second Language Acquisition*, we lay out the theories of second-language acquisition and showed how teachers translate those theories into practice. *Teaching Reading and Writing in Spanish in the Bilingual Classroom* reviews methods of teaching reading in Spanish and shows how reading and writing can develop in two languages when teachers use current, theoretically sound approaches to instruction. In *ESL/EFL Teaching: Principles for Success*, we outline the different methods that have been used to teach English learners, introduce a checklist of effective practices for second-language teaching, and give examples of teachers who follow those practices. Finally, in *Teaching Reading in Multilingual Classrooms*, we present a checklist for effective reading that teachers can use with English learners of different ages and at different levels of English proficiency.

This book turns to the challenge of educating older struggling English learners. There are many of these students in schools across the country, and teachers have asked how to help them. No quick fix can be offered because language development takes time. It takes skilled teachers who use research-based methods to help students catch up. In this book, we review the pertinent research and offer examples of teachers who work successfully with older English learners, and we present four keys for working effectively with these students. We hope that this book will inform the practice of teachers in many schools as they face the challenge of educating older English learners.

Older Struggling
English Learners

Last spring Juan, Pepe, and María decided to go to the United States to be with their families. They wanted to have a better life and to get a better education. The three kids said good bye to their grandmothers. María cried because she was sad. The boys gathered clothes, slingshot, a knife, a rope, blankets, a flashlight, a map and compass. María was cooking and buying food for the three of them. They were excited about the trip.

This piece of writing is part of a several-pages-long language-experience story written collaboratively by fourth-, fifth-, and sixth-grade students in Sandra Mercuri's newcomer class. Sandra begins each year with a unit on immigration because she wants her students to connect their lives to the school curriculum as they develop academic English. She also wants them to develop a broader worldview and new concepts, so the students learn about the many different reasons immigrants come to this country, where they come from, and the ways they arrive. Sandra's approach is particularly critical because all her students are newly arrived English learners and most have had little formal schooling in their native languages.

Although these students lack the academic experiences of other students their age, they do not lack life experiences, so Sandra is sure to draw on their background knowledge. The story that the students wrote together reflects the real-life experiences of some of them. The following response was written by one of Sandra's students, Jesus, after he heard Sandra read *How Many Days to America?* (Bunting 1988), the story of an immigrant family that comes to America to escape a military dictatorship. Sandra uses this story during the immigration unit.

> Yo llege por le serro caminando con mi aguelito y con mi tio. Cuando curzamos el serro estava lloviendo. Y tanbie vinimo por la via del tren y tanbie cruzamos una carretera y nos escondimos mientra vinia la ben entonces llego la ben y entonces nos subimos a la ven escostados para que no nos agarrara la migra del camino y me trajiero para la casa.

> (Translation) I came through the hills walking with my grandpa and my uncle. When we crossed the hill it was raining. And we also came along the railroad track, and we also crossed a highway and we hid when the van was coming then the van arrived and then we lay down on the van's floor so the highway patrol wouldn't get us and they brought me to my house. (Mercuri 2000, 114)

Though Jesus' writing lacks conventional spelling and punctuation, he is able to describe his experience in clear writing. Others of Sandra's students are less proficient in their native language, and a few come to her class not knowing how to write at all. When non–English speaking students arrive in our schools without having had adequate schooling experiences in their native languages, they present special challenges to teachers.

Older students with limited formal schooling (LFS) like Jesus struggle to close the academic achievement gap. A second group of struggling older students we refer to as long-term English learners (LTELs). These are students who have been in this country for several years, but who have not developed high levels of literacy in either their first language or in English. Marisol is typical of this second group.

Marisol was born in a village in Michoacan, Mexico. She has six brothers and four sisters. Marisol attended kindergarten in Mexico, but she did not go to school the following year. When she and her family moved to a small, rural town in the United States, she was put into second grade. Her father, a farmworker, and her mother, a homemaker, put a high value on

Marisol's schooling. Despite their support, school in her new country has not been easy. Marisol remembers her first days of school in the United States. She wrote about that experience in her high school English class:

> When I started Washington school I was so nearveos becaue I didn't know anybody and I didn't understand anything in English.

For the next five years, Marisol received one hour of pullout ESL daily, but she didn't receive any first-language support.

Marisol is now in high school. Oscar, Marisol's ninth-grade English and reading teacher, was surprised that she had been in the United States so long. Her oral and written English proficiency is similar to that of more recent immigrants. He noticed that she especially lacks the academic language needed for schooling. But her progress in his class has been impressive, as Oscar's comments about her recent work show: "Marisol's work is greatly improved. I see confidence in her writing. She understands some of the ambiguities of the language, especially with poetry."

Just before the end of the year, Marisol told Oscar this:

> My mom saw me reading at home, and she asked me, "Is that homework?" and I said, "No, I'm just reading because I want to." I couldn't believe it myself. I usually would watch TV or listen to the radio, but now I actually get into the books.

Oscar and Sandra have achieved success with at least some of their older English learners by using research-based approaches that have been shown to produce positive results. Our goal in this book is to describe the similarities and differences among the types of older English learners in U.S. schools, to review the research on effective programs for these students, and to provide many examples of successful classroom practice from teachers like Oscar and Sandra. It is our hope that this information will better prepare both new and veteran teachers to work more effectively with their older struggling English learners.

Types of English Learners

The range of backgrounds of English learners in upper-elementary, middle, and secondary schools is phenomenal and seldom recognized. Programs designed to help these students are often based on the assumption that all the students are alike. A look at three groups of older English learners presents a picture of their differences and similarities (Olsen and Jaramillo 1999). Figure 1–1 summarizes the characteristics of these three types of English learners.

The first group includes students who have come to this country within the last five years and who have strong educational backgrounds and literacy in their first language, and sometimes in other languages as well. They have developed academic language and skills in their first language that will transfer to their content-area studies in English. However, although many have studied English in their native countries, most lack conversational flu-

Type of Learner	Characteristics
Newly Arrived with Adequate Schooling	• Recent arrival (less than five years in U.S.) • Adequate schooling in native country • Soon catches up academically • May still score low on standardized tests given in English
Newly Arrived with Limited Formal Schooling	• Recent arrival (less than five years in U.S.) • Interrupted or limited schooling in native country • Limited native-language literacy • Below grade level in math • Poor academic achievement
Long-Term English Learner	• Seven or more years in U.S. • Below grade level in reading and writing • False perception of academic achievement • Adequate grades but low test scores • ESL or bilingual instruction, but no consistent program

FIGURE 1–1. *Types of Older English Learners (adapted from Olsen and Jaramillo 1999)*

ency in English. These students often do well in course work, though they struggle for several years to compete with native English speakers on standardized tests. These new arrivals fit into traditionally organized ESL (English as a second language) or ELD (English language development) programs and often are integrated into the mainstream after one or two years.

A second group of older students who are recent arrivals in this country come to school with interrupted or limited-formal-schooling backgrounds as well as limited English proficiency. They come from isolated, rural communities with few school facilities, if any; from refugee camps that often lack schools; from countries where war is commonplace; and from home life situations that have moved them frequently from place to place (Hamayan 1994).

Because of their limited-school experiences, these students struggle with reading and writing in their first language, or do not read or write their native language at all. In addition, they lack basic concepts in different subject areas. They are often at least two years below grade level in math. These students are faced with the complex task of developing conversational English, becoming literate in English, and gaining the academic knowledge and skills they need to compete academically with native English speakers. They do not have the academic background to draw upon in their native languages, so these students often struggle with course work and do not score well on standardized tests. They also lack an understanding of how schools are organized and how students are expected to act in schools. They are not familiar with school culture.

The English learners in the third group have been in U.S. schools for seven or more years. Indeed, many are high school students who attended kindergarten here. Usually, they have been in and out of various ESL or bilingual programs without ever having benefited from any kind of consistent support program. They also have often missed school for extended periods at different times. These LTELs are below grade level in reading and writing, and usually in math as well. They often get passing grades—Cs and even sometimes Bs—when they do the required work. Because teachers may be passing them simply because they turn in the work, their grades give many of these students a false perception of their academic achievement. When these students try to pass high school exit exams or when they take standardized tests, their scores are low. Most have conversational fluency in English but lack the academic English language proficiency they need to compete with native English speakers.

The first group of students, the newly arrived English learners with adequate first-language schooling, need support. They need effective bilingual or ESL programs that will allow them to continue to develop subject-matter knowledge and skills as they acquire English. They need knowledgeable teachers who can make English instruction comprehensible. They also need support as they go through culture shock and the adjustments involved in living in a new country and speaking a new language.

Although these traditional ESL students need specialized instruction, the other two groups face greater challenges in trying to succeed academically in a new country and a new language. For that reason, in this book we focus on students in the last two groups. We analyze their needs, outline the kind of curriculum that works best for them, and provide examples from classrooms of teachers like Sandra and Oscar who have worked successfully with them. Increasingly, the English learners in our schools come from these two groups.

Immigrant and Involuntary Minority Students

One important difference between limited-formal-schooling students and long-term English learners is sociocultural in nature because it has to do with the relationships that develop between social groups. Even though many students in both these groups come from families that live under difficult socioeconomic conditions, there are some significant differences between them. This difference is captured by the distinction Ogbu (1991) makes between *immigrant minorities* and *involuntary minorities.*

Like LFS students, immigrant minorities are recent arrivals. They are not generally influenced by the attitudes and values of the mainstream society because they measure their success by the standards of their homeland. New students from the Sudan, for example, might be from families that live in poverty by U.S. standards, but whose living conditions are much better than what they were in Africa.

Immigrant minorities are motivated by the belief that they can go back to their homeland and use the skills and academic degrees they earn in the United States. In addition, they can alternate their behavior between home and school. For example, Sikh students from India often take on some aspects of Western dress in school and speak English there. In school, they can dress and act in ways that would not be appropriate at home. At home, they have to dress, speak, and act according to their cultural norms. However, alternating behavior between home and school is not something that immigrant minorities find difficult. They assume that they must do this to succeed in the school world and still maintain their cultural traditions and values.

Ogbu also points out that the cultural differences between immigrant minorities and those in the cultural mainstream are *primary* differences that existed before the cultures came into contact. These differences are specific and easy to identify. They include such things as language, food, customs, and clothing. Immigrant minority members recognize these differences and work to overcome them if they believe that will lead to school success. Immigrant minorities succeed in schools at a higher rate than involuntary minorities do, and they operate on what Ogbu calls a folk theory for success—a belief that education leads to success—and so put a high value on education.

In contrast, involuntary minorities, like many LTELs, have lived in this country for years—often for generations. As a result, they are highly influenced by majority-group attitudes and values and measure success by mainstream standards. They cannot export skills or academic degrees to a distant homeland, and they can't alternate dress or behavior between school and home.

According to Ogbu, involuntary minorities are characterized by *secondary* cultural differences. These are differences that developed after the cultures came into contact, and they are more a matter of style than content. They might include ways of walking, talking, or dressing that are designed to signal identity in a particular group. Since the differences are intended to indicate distinctions between the minority group and members of mainstream culture, involuntary minorities do not alternate their behavior: They act the same way at school and outside school.

In many cases, involuntary minority members develop a folk theory for success that puts a low value on education. Successful members of involuntary minority groups generally move away from the area where they grew up, so they don't serve as positive role models for other group members. Involuntary minorities, then, do not see that education improves life's conditions, and they see few (if any) examples of success related to education. Not surprisingly, involuntary minorities have higher rates of school failure than immigrant minorities do.

Ogbu's theory helps to account for differences in the school performance of English learners. However, Valdés (1996) points out that it is difficult to categorize some groups as either immigrant or involuntary minorities. For example, among students of Mexican origin, there are both immigrant and involuntary minorities. Valdés argues that Mexican immigrants can be considered involuntary minorities when they

1. become conscious that they are no longer like Mexican nationals who have remained in Mexico,
2. feel little identification with these Mexican nationals,
3. self-identify as "Americans,"
4. become aware that as persons of Mexican origin they have a low status among the majority society, and
5. realize the permanent limitations they will encounter as members of this group. (26)

When people view themselves as Americans who are placed in low-status positions in society because of their backgrounds, they begin to develop the secondary cultural differences that Ogbu lists. These differences may be formed in opposition to mainstream institutions. When the mainstream institution in question is school, that opposition contributes to a pattern of school failure.

Like Valdés, Cummins (2000) has argued that an important determinant of school success or failure is the relative social status of various groups and their perception of their position in the social hierarchy. He has proposed a framework that focuses on the relationships of power among social groups. He suggests that schools use a transformative, intercultural orientation that would allow them to create collaborative relations of power between groups. In schools that adopt this orientation, power is not solely in the hands of school authorities. Rather, the school and community groups collaborate in decision making and share power. This orientation results in adding students' languages and cultures to the school curriculum, encouraging parents of all groups to become involved in the school, using transformative models of teaching, and adopting types of assessment that show what students can do. We have elaborated on Cummins' model and provided examples of teachers who take an intercultural orientation in *Between Worlds* (Freeman and Freeman 2001).

Although some groups, such as students of Mexican origin, are difficult to classify, Ogbu's distinction between immigrant and involuntary minorities helps explain the social factors that contribute to the school performance of English learners. Researchers have pointed out that the distinction does not account for the performance of some groups, the differences within groups, or some other variables, such as socioeconomic differences. However, most researchers agree that Ogbu's insights are valuable.

Ogbu's theory is based on sociocultural factors. Purcell-Gates (1995), like other researchers, explains the importance of taking a sociocultural perspective. She studied an urban Appalachian family in which the parents were not literate. Purcell-Gates notes that the failure of minority groups, including the poor whites she studied, is often attributed to cognitive factors or to the assumption that the cultural group is deficient in some way. She argues that such explanations come from a mainstream perspective on reality that holds that all groups should value the same things that the mainstream group values. Purcell-Gates says that we can only understand the poor academic achievement of certain groups by understanding how they view the world and the place of school within their world. This approach, like Ogbu's, is a sociocultural one. Purcell-Gates writes:

> It is this sociocultural theoretical lens, I believe, that offers us the best chance of understanding the low literacy attainment by poor and minority peoples. How can we understand why so many children do not learn what the mainstream schools think they are teaching unless we can get "inside" the learners and see the world through their eyes? If we do not try to do this, if we continue to use the mainstream experience of reality as the perspective, we fool ourselves into believing that we are looking through a window when instead we are looking into a mirror. Our explanations threaten to reflect only ourselves and our world, serving no real explanatory purpose. (6)

Ogbu's sociocultural theory includes the perceptions of the members of the two groups toward the mainstream. Both groups experience discriminatory treatment, but they react to that experience differently. Immigrant minorities expect poor treatment, largely ignore or discount it, and find ways to succeed despite obstacles.

In contrast, involuntary minorities are very aware of prejudicial treatment. Members resent discriminatory treatment and develop ways to oppose it. Involuntary minorities generally put a low value on education, but immigrants see school as the key to success. By considering the perceptions of the two groups—the way they view reality—instead of assuming that they see things the same way the mainstream does, one can better account for their school performance.

In many ways, the distinction Ogbu makes between immigrant and involuntary minorities parallels our classification of English learners into two groups: those who are recent arrivals with limited formal schooling and those who are long-term English learners. Many of the LFS students have all the characteristics of immigrant minorities. Most LTELs would fall into Ogbu's involuntary minority group. This difference is important for teachers to take into account. For example, effective teachers of LTELs devote considerable time helping their students learn to value school and to begin to see themselves as successful learners.

Mary, a high school teacher, read Ogbu's theory and then reflected on her own students in two different schools. The students she identified as immigrants were recent arrivals who came to the high school with limited formal schooling. In contrast, those she identified as involuntary minorities were her long-term English learners:

> Through my teaching experiences, I have seen that Ogbu's theory is a reality. A clear example is seen in the ELD [English Language Development] classes of both high schools I have worked in. It was and has been my observation that students in ELD level one fit the characteristics of immigrant minorities.
>
> When asked, these students will explain that they have come to the United States because they know there are better opportunities here. Although they have problems adjusting to the culture and language, they work hard and do fairly well in school. For the most part, these students move quickly through the ELD program and into mainstream classes. These students realize that their situation is not easy and is often unfair, yet they feel that they have it better here in the U.S. than they would in their home country.
>
> Some of the involuntary students I have worked with were my ELD level four students in the first school where I taught. Many of the students had been in the United States many years, some were even born here. They viewed the dominant society as having all of the power and saw that minorities face discrimination and unjust treatment as well as having little if any opportunity of academic success. They had no role models and saw very few minorities succeed. Most of the minorities from the community that did succeed left the community. Therefore, these students were not able to see their academic success put into practice.
>
> These students were not sure that education leads to success. They had distrust for school, which is a white-controlled institution. For the most part, these students had long ago given up the idea that they could be successful in school and in their lives.

One factor that Ogbu's classification fails to take into account is the prior schooling of students within the immigrant group. New immigrants with adequate formal schooling succeed at higher rates in schools in the United States than new immigrants with limited or interrupted schooling. The latter group faces a much greater challenge. Nevertheless, Ogbu's distinction between immigrant and involuntary minorities helps provide a clearer picture of the struggling older English learners in our schools. As recent demographic studies show, the number of English learners has increased dramatically in recent years.

English Language Learners in Schools

According to the National Clearinghouse of Bilingual Education, 4.1 million students in the United States are classified as limited English proficient. Among these students, there is great diversity in languages and countries of national origin. Though the vast majority, 72.9 percent, speak Spanish, the diversity even among Spanish speakers is great. The 2000 census reports that 66.1 percent of the 35.3 million Hispanics living in the United States are from Mexico. Others come from Central and South America, Puerto Rico, Cuba, and other Spanish-speaking countries, and they have different cultural backgrounds and speak different varieties of Spanish (Barone 2001).

While the terms *Hispanic, Latino,* and *Latina* are generally used to describe these students, this blanket designation may prevent teachers from recognizing the diversity within their classrooms. For example, all of Sandra's students come from Mexico, but many do not speak Spanish as their first language. Instead, they speak Trique or Mixteco, indigenous Mexican Indian languages. Even when all the students in a particular classroom have Spanish as a first language, significant differences exist. In fact, as Jiménez (2001) points out, many educators lump all Latinos together even though these students are very aware that their roots are in different countries and different traditions. In addition, those born in the United States know that they differ not only from mainstream students of European American origin, but also from new immigrants. Our son-in-law, Francisco, arrived here from El Salvador at age fourteen. He still remembers how his culture shock was heightened by the fact that everyone he came in contact with—his teachers, his peers, and even his coaches—assumed he was from Mexico.

According to Canedy (2001), Hispanic students make up the largest majority of English learners. In California, for example, almost 80 percent of the students identified as English learners are Spanish speaking. Many do well academically, but the dropout rate is higher among California's Hispanic students than in any other group. Thirty-one percent of the Hispanic boys drop out, compared to 12.1 percent of African American boys and 7.7 percent of Anglo boys. Twenty-six percent of the Hispanic girls drop out, compared with 13 percent of African American girls and 6.9 percent of Anglo girls.

Canedy also points out that while many of the reasons these students drop out are related to social and economic conditions, their previous educational experiences are also a factor:

> Many Hispanic immigrants are either economic refugees from Mexico or war refugees from Central America. Thus, they come to this country very often with little schooling. (A3)

Certainly, not all immigrant students are Spanish speaking. After Spanish, the top language groups in U.S. schools are Vietnamese, Hmong, Cantonese, and Cambodian. Like Hispanics, Asian students differ considerably from one another. They speak different languages and come from different cultural traditions. In addition, there are differences in the academic achievement of Asian students. Chang (2001) found that while some Asian students do very well academically, others do not.

> Asian American students are often perceived as college-bound and model minority students; however, Asian Pacific American student populations differ significantly in socioeconomic status, education aspirations, English language proficiency, optimal learning opportunities, or family/community support. (17)

The research that Chang conducted shows that many Asians, even those who began school as kindergartners in the U.S., reach sixth grade with low academic skills and a reading ability three or four grade levels below that of their peers.

In a 2000 report that reviewed research on English learners in U.S. schools, G. García and colleagues identify some key concerns. They report that these students are less likely than mainstream students to have had the kind of early pre-reading supports that teachers expect, such as being read aloud to, using educational games and toys, inventing stories, and reciting rhymes. Certainly, refugee children have probably had little opportunity for such experiences. In addition, the researchers found that English learners as a group often live in households and neighborhoods with high and sustained poverty, so their lives are extremely complex and school is not always the first priority. Meeting basic needs becomes a key concern.

Among English language learners living in challenging settings, some seem to be more successful than others. Those who do well despite their circumstances have been termed "resilient." Researchers are identifying individual and school processes that lead to and foster success for nonresilient English learners (Wang, Haertel, and Walberg 1994; Winfield 1991; Padrón, Waxman, Brown, and Powers 2000). Padrón and colleagues, for example, found that resilient English learners use their native language at home and with friends more frequently than nonresilient students do. They also found that 44 percent of the nonresilient students had repeated at least one grade, while only 11 percent of the resilient students were held back a year, leading one to question whether retention is effective for students acquiring English.

The impact of older English learners on U.S. schools continues to grow. Fleischman and Hopstock (1993) estimate that 20 percent of those identified as English learners in high schools and 12 percent of those in middle school have missed two or more years of schooling. With over a million more English learners in schools now than in 1993, teachers must be prepared to work with the large number of English learners who have had limited or interrupted schooling, are long-term English learners, or are nonresilient students. The literature suggests that these students are poorly understood and are not adequately served by schools (G. García 2000). But despite these sobering reports, some teachers are working very effectively with all types of English learners.

Assessing and Placing Students

As the number of English learners increases, it becomes more important to develop adequate methods for assessing and placing them. When David taught in a small high school in the early 1970s, some new students who did not speak very much English arrived. Since David had lived in Latin America, he was tapped to assess these Spanish speakers. The assessment was quite informal. Since there were no bilingual or ESL classes at the school, the students were placed in the lower-track (nonacademic) classes.

Times have changed. States have requirements for assessing students, and in most districts a specialist oversees testing and placement. The school or district may even have an intake center and a newcomer school to accommodate new arrivals with limited English proficiency. Schools administer surveys to determine what languages are spoken in students' homes, and for students who speak a language other than English, schools follow up with one or more tests.

Even though things are better now than when David first tried to determine the needs and abilities of the students who came to his school, many schools rely exclusively on oral language tests of English proficiency. Carrasquillo and Rodríguez (1996) explain why this is a problem:

> An examination of mainstream instructional demands yields a listing of content area topics, thinking skills, and linguistic domains necessary for learning, not necessarily assessed through the above instruments [home language survey and oral language proficiency tests]. (31)

Oral language tests fail to measure students' ability to read and write. The state of California realized this limitation with tests they were using and developed the CELDT (California English Language Development Test) to assess reading, speaking, and writing skills and to provide information to determine levels of English proficiency. However, teachers and resource personnel have reported that the exam is proving to be a challenge to administer and to interpret and still does not provide information about students' background knowledge in academic content areas.

Carrasquillo and Rodríguez suggest the use of multidimensional assessment procedures including the following:

(a) information from teachers or teachers' referrals,
(b) information from parents,
(c) evaluation of records,
(d) appraisal of the student's academic level, and
(e) appraisal of the student's language skills. (32)

The authors point out that schools need to use a variety of instruments to assess students' language proficiency and content knowledge. Clearly, such assessment is a schoolwide or districtwide task. It involves collecting information from teachers and parents, as well as administering various types of tests. Carrasquillo and Rodríguez offer several helpful suggestions and forms that teachers can use for assessing students.

For some students, it is quite difficult to locate records of previous schooling. Since many new arrivals are experiencing culture shock, tests given soon after they arrive may not produce accurate results. Once students are assessed and placed, it is important for teachers to observe them carefully to confirm that their placement is appropriate. A very useful handbook that can serve as a resource for teachers is *Performance and Portfolio Assessment for Language Minority Students,* by Pierce and O'Malley (1992). This book contains a number of rubrics and other instruments for collecting and evaluating data about the language proficiency of English learners.

Mace-Matluck and colleagues (1998) point out that "Early identification of immigrant adolescents with limited prior schooling is necessary so that students' needs may be served as effectively as possible" (108). They hold that schools must evaluate prior schooling and native-language proficiency as well as English proficiency. They also suggest that schools find out about the schooling of parents and siblings to determine the kinds of support students can receive at home.

For many schools, assessing students' native-language proficiency is especially difficult. In our local district in Fresno, California, for example, home language surveys have identified more than one hundred different languages, and school personnel are not available to evaluate some of those languages. Schools can involve parents and other community members in the evaluation process. As Mace-Matluck and colleagues state, "Assessment of native language literacy is a crucial factor in the intake process, because prior schooling in the home country does not guarantee students' proficiency in academic language" (109). Although it may be a challenge for schools to find ways to evaluate students' literacy skills in their native languages, that information is crucial because first-language literacy and content knowledge are strong predictors of academic success in English.

Assessing English learners is a complex task, and all too often when new students arrive, teachers are not provided with all the information they need to plan effective instruction. Assessment should be a schoolwide or districtwide concern. Accurate assessment and placement is important if students are to receive appropriate educational services. When David carried out a very informal evaluation of the new arrivals at his school, the school had only a handful of limited-English-proficient students and no real place to put them. Now, all across the country, schools are faced with assessing and placing increasing numbers of English learners in educational settings that will support their academic success. Once placed, English learners need specialized instruction that will help them succeed academically.

Four Keys for School Success for Older English Learners

We have developed four key ideas to help teachers implement effective practices for working with older English learners (Figure 1–2).

The first key is to engage students in a challenging curriculum. Even though many students with limited formal schooling and many long-term English learners have not developed the academic concepts and language proficiency of other students their age, they are capable. What they need are activities that will stretch them. Effective teachers organize their curriculum around themes based on big questions designed to push students' thinking. Without a challenging curriculum, older English learners will not develop the academic English they need to close the achievement gap.

The second key is to build on what students bring to the learning situation. There may be a gap between what the schools expect and what students bring, but that does not mean that these students do not bring anything. They each have a language, a culture, and background experiences. Effective teachers draw on these resources and build new concepts on this strong experiential base.

The third key is to scaffold instruction. It is not helpful to offer challenging curriculum without also providing the support that students need to

Four Keys for School Success
1. Engage students in challenging, theme-based curriculum to develop academic concepts.
2. Draw on students' background—their experiences, cultures, and languages.
3. Organize collaborative activities and scaffold instruction to build students' academic English proficiency.
4. Create confident students who value school and value themselves as learners.

FIGURE 1–2. *Four Keys for School Success for Older English Learners*

engage with lessons. One way teachers do this is by organizing collaborative activities and providing other means to scaffold instruction.

The fourth key is to create confident learners. Older, struggling English learners often lack confidence. They may not see themselves as capable. They may not understand how schools work, or they may have concluded that schooling does not offer them any benefits. Effective teachers help all their students value school and value themselves as learners.

Three Effective Teachers

Sandra

Sandra Mercuri is a bilingual Spanish/English teacher and a recent immigrant from Argentina. She feels that being an immigrant helps her understand her students, even though her experience has been very different from theirs. Sandra's students are fourth, fifth, and sixth graders living in a rural farming community in California. Almost all are newcomers to this country and speak either Spanish or one of two native dialects of southern Mexico, Mixteco and Trique. They arrive here with little or no previous schooling, and often come to Sandra's classroom unfamiliar with school routines and expectations. Only a few are literate in their first language, and most lack confidence in themselves as learners.

Since many of the children are from migrant families, their schooling, once they start studying in the United States, often continues to be interrupted. Work takes families north for several months each year and family obligations take them back to Mexico for Christmas. The composition of Sandra's class is constantly changing. Only a few students stay with her for an entire semester, let alone the whole year. Other teachers often ask Sandra to take students into her classroom because they don't know what to do with or for them. Sandra's challenge is to provide these students with the literacy skills and concept development they have missed and help them develop enough academic English to survive in junior high and high school. She understands that to do this, she must help them build self-confidence and pride in themselves, their culture, and their language.

Sandra has prepared herself well to work with these students. In her native Argentina, she studied language acquisition and has the equivalent of a master's degree in Spanish linguistics. Upon arriving in the United States, she got her teaching credential at a small university that is known for its innovative teacher-education program, then continued into a graduate program where she earned a bilingual/cross-cultural specialist credential, as well as an M.A. in bilingual/cross-cultural education. Sandra specialized in students with limited formal schooling, choosing that topic for her thesis. Since completing the M.A., Sandra has conducted research with Yvonne on effective practices for limited-formal-schooling students. She has also collaborated with Yvonne on several professional presentations and articles. Sandra now works as an adjunct professor at the university from which she graduated. Recently, she was chosen as one of three finalists for Teacher of the Year among all the districts in her county.

Oscar

Oscar Hernández was born and raised in the central valley of California. His parents were farmworkers, and he worked in the fields himself. Oscar remembers his experiences in high school, when he and other Hispanic students often felt mistreated and left out.

As he was growing up, Oscar found support from his Hispanic church and connected with his Mexican roots through involvement in Mexican folkloric dance and music. Supported by his church, he went to a small Christian college. There he made friends with other students and members of the faculty. He earned his B.A. and then got his teaching credential. Oscar has now taught for seven years. He has worked at various grade levels in several school districts. Recently, he took a teaching position near his hometown, where he works with mostly Hispanic freshmen who have been identified as struggling readers.

Through the college he attended, Oscar became involved with experienced mentors who have helped him develop creative and innovative literacy practices for his secondary students. He has worked with a secondary teacher, Pam Smith, on a literacy teacher–training team in one district and formed a continuing professional relationship with this knowledgeable mentor. He also received training in The Learning Edge, a program developed by Bobbi Jentes Mason in which high school and entering college students receive an intensive two-week literacy experience. Most of the students who participate in The Learning Edge have had interrupted formal schooling or are long-term English learners.

Oscar's experiences on the literacy-training team and in The Learning Edge, as well as his current studies in an M.A. reading program, have prepared him not only to meet the needs of his high school students, but also to present his classroom and curriculum to other secondary teachers at in-services and conferences.

Grace

Grace Klassen is an experienced junior high school teacher with a real heart for teaching and meeting her diverse students' needs. About half of her students are Anglo and the other half are Latino. Grace teaches eighth graders and puts a great deal of time and effort into getting to know her students and caring for them. Although Grace doesn't speak Spanish, she understands her students' academic and cultural needs. She took courses in second-language acquisition to prepare herself to work more effectively with her English learners, and is completing an M.A. in reading. In her thesis, Grace describes an extensive unit on diversity that she has developed with her students.

The community Grace teaches in has a population of about eight thousand. While much of the town's income is based on agriculture, recently the town has become popular with tourists. The quaint downtown was remodeled and several antique shops have become popular. There is a large mural depicting the diverse people who make up the community, including Native Americans, Mexican immigrants, and Anglos.

While the downtown has been refurbished and appears to welcome diversity, there are definitely sections of town that are economically depressed where a large number of the Mexican-origin citizens live. One large section is known for gang activity and poverty. Many of Grace's students live in this part of town. The people of this area have little voice in the community or in the schools.

Grace sees her teaching as a vocation and puts time and dedication into planning for her students. Over the last five years, she has been instrumental in encouraging eighth-grade teachers at her school to plan together in order to give students a more integrated curriculum experience. She works especially closely with a social studies teacher to connect American history to literature and writing around the topic of American folkways.

Grace is extremely respectful of her students and their lives. Daily, she greets them at the door, shakes their hands, and welcomes them. Her students often share personal news, concerns, and successes with Grace during this time. Together with the time she spends reading and researching, this sharing gives Grace the information she needs to draw on the background experiences her students bring to the classroom. Grace works to connect her teaching to her students' reality, finding readings and developing units that will be relevant and meaningful to them. The title of her master's thesis shows this clearly: "Making Real the Promise of Democracy: Valuing All Voices Through Stories of Diversity."

Sandra, Oscar, and Grace are only three teachers among many we have worked with over the years. Their classrooms and their classroom practices are described in detail in the following chapters because their students are limited-formal-schooling or long-term English learners, and their teaching exemplifies the research-based principles of effective teaching for English language learners that we advocate.

We hope that readers of this book will be able to visualize the classrooms and activities we describe and see how the activities might be applied to the classrooms and students they know. Our goal is for this book to help those charged with educating English learners to put research-based theory into practice.

Professional Extensions

1. Investigate the English-learner population in your school and district. How many students have been identified as being English learners? What are the primary languages represented among them? How has the population of English learners changed over the past five years? The past ten years?
2. How does the population of English learners in your district compare with the population in the rest of your state? In the United States?
3. How have your state, district, and school responded to the needs of English learners? What kinds of programs are available? How are teachers prepared?
4. Do your school and district make a distinction among the different kinds of older English learners described in this chapter? If so, how do they do so? If not, do you see a need for such a distinction? Why? Why not?
5. Review the discussion of immigrant minority and involuntary minority students. Identify a student you believe might fit one of the two groups, then interview the student. Does this student fit into one of the categories? How or how not?

6. Cummins says that schools should use a transformative, intercultural orientation to address the needs of English learners. Purcell-Gates says that schools should look at students through a sociocultural theoretical lens. Does your school have a transformative, intercultural orientation? What programs are in place for English learners? What changes, if any, would you suggest to improve educational opportunities for English learners at your school?
7. How are English learners assessed and placed in your school and district? What labels are they given? How do the labels affect attitudes about the students?
8. Review the four keys for school success for older English learners. To what degree does your teaching or the teaching in a classroom you have observed follow these keys? How could that teaching be changed to more closely reflect the keys?

What Older English Learners Need

Older English learners who struggle in school may be characterized in a number of ways. For example, we could look at their primary languages and cultures or their social and economic conditions. These factors all play a role in the academic achievement of older English learners. Forces from both the social context and the school context interact with individual student characteristics in complex ways (Cortés 1986). These interactions help shape the academic performance of English learners.

This book focuses on two groups of struggling older English learners. The first group is made up of recent arrivals with limited formal schooling. The second group consists of students who have lived in the United States for many years without developing grade-level-appropriate academic English or content-area knowledge and skills. Students in both groups come from a variety of linguistic and cultural backgrounds. Most of the students in both groups live in difficult social and economic conditions.

We listed the characteristics of each group in Chapter 1 (see Figure 1–1). In this chapter we describe students who are representative of the two groups, and we discuss an important aspect of their language development: the distinction between conversational and academic language. We examine the similarities between students in these two groups, as well as their differences. Some students clearly fit one of the categories, but other students are more difficult to categorize. Nevertheless, general patterns emerge, and an increased awareness of the differences among older English learners can enable teachers to plan appropriate instruction for them.

Limited-Formal-Schooling Students

In Chapter 1 we included a response to an immigrant story written by Jesus, one of Sandra's students. Jesus is typical of Sandra's students, many of whom fall into the limited formal schooling (LFS) category of English learners. They are recent arrivals who have either not attended school or whose schooling has been interrupted. The following sections describe some of Sandra's students, and other students who fit the LFS category.

Adelaida

"Why should I try? I'm going away again." These were eleven-year-old Adelaida's words when her teacher, Sandra, asked why she wasn't participating in activities with her group. In just a week Adelaida was leaving for Oregon again as she had done two years before. Last year, she had stayed all year in Sandra's class, and her teacher was really beginning to see progress. Adelaida was gaining confidence as a student. Her reading and writing in English were improving, and she was showing an understanding of the key concepts she had been studying in the thematic units Sandra teaches.

Adelaida's family usually works the crops in California from January to April. Then they go to Oregon from May to October to pick cherries and apples. During November and December they travel to Mexico to visit relatives and celebrate the holidays. Last year, as a ten year old, Adelaida had stayed in California to take care of her ailing father and younger siblings, who were in kindergarten and second grade, while her mother and older brothers and sisters went to Oregon.

This year, however, the whole family was going to Oregon, where Adelaida and her siblings all work and do not attend school. They need the money, and the climate is better for their father, who has been diagnosed with asthma. In the central valley of California the dust and insecticides have ruined his health. He has become so ill that he needs to carry an oxygen tank with him at all times, and he can no longer work there.

Adelaida has many responsibilities for a girl her age. She gets up every morning at four to help her mother cook for the family. She often works weekends in the fields, especially in the high season, to augment the family income. Last year she served as the language broker when her father, who speaks no English, was in the hospital and the rest of the family was in Oregon.

Sandra realized that this move would be almost the last straw for Adelaida. Because she is getting older and stayed in school last year, Adelaida knows how much she will miss while in Oregon. She also knows that next year is her sixth-grade year, and if the family goes to Oregon in May again, she will miss all the graduation activities, including sixth-grade camp and a much-looked-forward-to trip to an amusement park.

Sandra tried to encourage Adelaida before she left. She reminded her that her father was working on getting their legal papers, which would come soon. She also gave her a book to read and a journal to write in. She told her, "I want you to read this book and write letters to me. Keep a journal. I haven't been in Oregon." Sandra was touched when Adelaida showed how she had learned to respond to readings by replying, "And I'll write who did what, when, and where!"

Adelaida is quite typical of students in the limited formal schooling (LFS) category. She has been in the United States less than five years. Her schooling was limited before she arrived and has been interrupted frequently since she has been in this country. She did not develop literacy in her first language and is below grade level in her academic subjects. She has considerable academic potential, but life circumstances have prevented her from realizing that potential.

Mario

Mario is another eleven year old. He came from Mexico to Sandra's class a little over a year ago. Next year he will be with her as a sixth grader. Mario had limited schooling in Mexico. For two years he lived in a *rancho*, a tiny rural village. There was a school in the rancho, but despite efforts to find someone, no teacher was willing to come teach there. Mario remembers going to the school several times, but each time he was sent home because the expected teacher had not arrived. Mario's father is very worried about this period of interrupted schooling. He knows his son is behind, and he has talked to Sandra several times about this. In fact, despite a very long workday, the father attends school two nights a week to learn English in the hope of being better able to help his children with their schoolwork.

Sandra provides support for her newcomer students by giving a preview of the lessons in Spanish, and this seems to be helping Mario. He listens well when Sandra teaches in English and is developing a good receptive understanding of his new language. Mario has plans for his future. He wants to join the army or become a fireman or a policeman. He showed a great deal of interest when a team teacher working with Sandra told him the army might help pay for his college education. He asked her several questions about this possibility.

Mario is very outgoing and an excellent storyteller. When studying different topics, he makes connections with his own experiences. Sandra smiles as she talks about Mario:

> He is always making connections with his culture. He talks about family ties and often begins a story with "Mi abuelito me contó" (My grandfather told me). He's funny and persistent. He entertains us all and is constantly telling me, "Oh, teacher, one more thing . . ."

Mario also seems typical of LFS students. His schooling in Mexico was extremely limited, so he did not develop literacy in his primary language. He arrived in the United States recently and is below grade level in his academic subjects. He is learning to speak English, but he is still more comfortable in Spanish. His parents are very supportive of his education, and he has a more stable home situation than Adelaida does. Nevertheless, he is far behind other fifth graders in academic content knowledge.

Seeham, Esmet, and Fatima

Seeham, Esmet, and Fatima are third-, fourth- and fifth-grade girls who came to school for the first time this year when school officials in their rural community discovered that their parents, conservative Muslim immigrants from Yemen, had been sending only the two boys in the family to school for the past two years. Girls normally stay at home in their tradition, so these three have had no schooling. They cannot read or write in their native language, and they speak very little English. Although they have lived in the United States for two years, they have been insulated from U.S. culture and the English language.

These Yemeni girls have all the characteristics of LFS students. The oldest, Seeham, has perhaps struggled the most. Her reading teacher, Sandy, explains how difficult things were when she first came to school:

> At first, she did not talk. However, she did appear to understand much of what I said. We came to an agreement. She would nod for "yes" and shake her head for "no." She would point and draw pictures. She was extremely nervous at first, and was even hesitant to draw. She kept erasing.

Certainly, these girls face tremendous challenges, as do their teachers.

There are other questions to consider for these girls. Although their parents are now sending them to school, the parents may not put great value on education for girls. With little home support and very limited academic English, these girls will need considerable support over several years to succeed in school.

Paj

Paj, a Hmong student studied by Vang (2000), came to the U.S. from Laos, where her early schooling had been interrupted by the war. Later, she attended school for a short time while living in a refugee camp. She now lives with her mother and four younger siblings in a two-bedroom inner-city apartment complex. At age thirteen she has many responsibilities, including caring for younger siblings. Paj has learned to speak English quite well, but she struggles academically. She hopes to graduate from high school, but that goal seems unrealistic given her problems with academic work, especially science and history. There is no one to help Paj with schoolwork when she needs it. She describes the hopelessness of her situation:

> If I don't do my homework, then I ask my Mom to sign her name to show that there was no one at home who could help me. The teacher doesn't care and I don't care.

Paj's last line is sobering. Since Vang did his research with her, Paj has left home, dropped out of school, and moved in with her boyfriend, who is a member of one of the local Hmong gangs.

Paj has been in the United States longer than the other students we have described, but she has been here fewer than five years. She has developed conversational English, but is considerably behind her classmates in academics. We place her in the LFS category because her early schooling was interrupted and she did not develop primary-language literacy. Her younger siblings might more easily fit into the long-term English learner category because they arrived in the United States when they were young enough to begin school here.

Francisca

Seventeen-year-old Francisca attended school in Mexico through the sixth grade. She came to this country four years ago at age thirteen with her mother and brother to work in the orchards in Oregon. At age fifteen, she met a young man and ran away with him to a city in California. Her mother reported her as a minor and Child Protective Services placed her in a foster home. Since then she has had a baby and has been in two foster homes and two continuation high schools. In the second continuation school she now attends, she has been placed as a ninth grader in a program for young mothers, where she takes both academic classes and child-rearing classes. Her English is quite limited, though she reads and writes Spanish and is picking up English fairly well considering her tremendous personal challenges.

Francisca is typical of students in the LFS category in some respects. She is a new arrival and most of her schooling was in Mexico. She developed native-language literacy. However, there was a gap in her schooling between the time she completed sixth grade and the time she started school in the U.S. and was placed in ninth grade. For that reason, she did not arrive with adequate formal education. Her schooling in the United States was also limited, first due to the demands of work, then as the result of her running off to California. She is behind her classmates academically and needs strong educational support to begin to catch up.

Long-Term English Learners

In Chapter 1 we described Marisol, one of Oscar's secondary students. Marisol has many of the characteristics of a second group of older struggling English learners. She has been in school in the United States for many years, but she is still limited in her academic English proficiency, and she has not done well in school. Many other students may be classified as long-term English learners. We describe some of them below.

José

José, another of Oscar's students, was born in Guadalajara, Mexico, and came to the United States when he was in first grade. He attended several rural elementary schools, then his family settled in the city where he now attends high school. His father is a farmworker and his mother is employed in a local fruit-packing house.

José had no preschool or kindergarten in Mexico. In the United States he was placed in English-only programs. He received no first-language support in any of the programs he attended. Although José can communicate socially in English, he still lacks academic English and at the end of his freshman year he remains a reluctant reader. Oscar hoped that he might find a "home-run book," a book that would get José excited about reading (Von Sprecken 2000). Even though José does not choose to read novels in his free time, he comprehends expository texts and is able to pick out main ideas quite easily.

In the past José has been involved with gangs. For one of his descriptive writing assignments he wrote graphically about a cousin who was killed while drunk after partying with his homeboys. Perhaps this is why José has made a decision to leave the gangs.

José likes to be called Junior. His nickname on the soccer team is *El Conejo* (The Rabbit), an apt name for someone who can run fast. He was elected most valuable player in the region. Oscar knows that he is beginning to make progress with José as a student because on the last day of school, when José and his friends would ordinarily leave quickly, they hung around Oscar's room chatting, drawing pictures of their teacher, and generally seeming reluctant to end the year.

José is typical of students in the LTEL category. He has been in the United States for most of his school years. However, he has not had a consistent program that would allow him to develop age-appropriate academic concepts while learning English. As a result, he is below grade level. With Oscar's help, José is beginning to catch up, but as with other older English learners, he faces the reality of having a limited time before he must take graduation exit exams.

Andrew

Andrew, a native-Chinese-speaking middle-school student who has attended schools in the San Francisco area since kindergarten, struggles in class and is reading four grade levels below his peers. Many Asian Pacific middle-school students like Andrew are being recommended for special education classes because they do not read at grade level. However, these special classes seldom address the needs of English language learners (Chang 2001).

Students like Andrew are typical of the LTEL category. They do not read and write in their primary language. In fact, all their schooling may have been in English. Their conversational ability in English is similar to that of a native speaker. Nevertheless, they have not developed academic English, and their school performance is well below average. They need academic support from teachers who are knowledgeable about second-language issues, but they do not need the kind of support designed for special education students.

Javier

Javier came to this country at age twelve when his mother, who for eight years had been a farmworker in California, was able to save enough money to arrange papers for him and his older brother. Javier had attended school only sporadically in El Salvador. He preferred to fish or hunt, and his grandmother and other extended family members with whom he lived did not object since he was putting food on the table. Once in the United States, Javier went to large, inner-city junior high and high schools and graduated. Although he did get through high school, the radical change from his surroundings in El Salvador to his life in the United States presented him with many challenges.

Javier's story is similar to that of many other Salvadoran refugees. Osterling (1998) explains that many newcomer Salvadoran students come from rural areas and have had limited formal educational opportunities. In U.S. schools

> these youngsters often found themselves in an environment where almost all teachers, students, and administrators spoke, dressed, and acted in a very different way. Therefore, the student's self-esteem and well-being was challenged from the outset. The beginning of their American school experience often also coincided with their family reunification, after being left back in El Salvador for many years with their grandparents, friends, or relatives while their parents earned enough money for their trip. (10, 11)

After graduation, Javier got a job at one of the high schools working with computers, and he now supervises others updating and maintaining the computer systems. He is self-taught with computers but does not feel capable of handling the reading and writing demands of college. Though he uses English at work, he is much more comfortable speaking Spanish.

Javier may appear to fit in the LFS category. His early schooling in El Salvador was limited, and when he began school in the United States he did not speak English and had not developed academic subject-matter knowledge. Although he could read and write in Spanish, his Spanish literacy was below grade level.

However, he more closely fits the LTEL category. He has now been in the United States more than five years. He never got the help of a consistent bilingual or ESL program, and he is behind academically even though he has developed specialized knowledge in the computer field. He was able to finish high school and now has a good job, but he has little incentive to continue his education.

Mireya

Fifteen-year-old Mireya was born to a single mother in San Bernardino, California, on a sidewalk next to her home. Most of her schooling has been in the small rural town where Grace, the teacher we introduced in Chapter 1, works. Mireya grew up in the section of town known for crime and poverty. Her older brothers and sisters are all members of a local gang. Until this year, in fact, Mireya was a known troublemaker, but she wrote Grace in a letter at the beginning of her eighth-grade year that she was going to be changing her path.

Mireya's academic performance up to the eighth grade was dismal. Her records showed frequent Fs. Mireya explained to Grace that early in her schooling others made fun of her for her accent and her struggles to learn English. She responded by striking back and out and making no effort in school. She now speaks both Spanish and English, but she has not developed grade-level academic proficiency in either language.

This year in Grace's class Mireya is doing a great deal of reading and writing. Though she is reading novels that are usually considered appropriate for younger students, including books in the *Boxcar Children* and *Little House on the Prairie* series, she is making excellent progress. Her comprehension is good, and she participates in class activities enthusiastically. She enjoys reading and writing and has a positive attitude toward school.

Mireya is typical of the LTEL category. All her schooling has been in the United States. She did not experience an academic program that allowed her to develop academic content knowledge in her first language while she was learning English. She never developed literacy in Spanish, and although she has conversational language proficiency in both languages, she has not developed academic language proficiency in either language.

María

Grace first felt she had connected with another of her students, María, during a unit on the Mexican celebration honoring family members who have died, *el Día de los Muertos* (the Day of the Dead). María shared how her mothers' death six years before had devastated her and was the beginning of the disintegration of her large family. María's home is known as a drug center and a place for wild parties. Her older siblings are gang members and recently an older brother was expelled from school.

María began sharing with Grace after talking about her mother. She told Grace how no one at home paid any attention to her and no one ever tried to help her. Her father works in the fields all day and doesn't know how to cope with his children. María was especially hurt when no one even noticed that her birthday had come and gone.

In earlier years, María attended rural schools in California wherever her father found work. Though her father and mother spoke only Spanish, she never learned to read and write in her first language. Now in junior high school, her academic work is below grade level. Grace notices that María has gaps in her knowledge of basic concepts, and that she often seems lost when given assignments.

Like Mireya, María is typical of students in the LTEL category. She began school in the United States. She did not have an effective bilingual or ESL program. Her early schooling was interrupted, and now her social situation affects her school performance. She has an excellent teacher in Grace, and she has developed a positive attitude toward school. However, she is behind academically and will need long-term support to catch up.

Teresa

Teresa is another LTEL student in Grace's eighth-grade language arts class. However, her story is somewhat different from the others. She has been in schools in the United States since kindergarten and speaks English well;

yet, according to her seventh-grade language arts teacher, she arrived in junior high school without being able to write sentences in English.

Teresa's parents are farmworkers who do not speak English. She is an only child, but has a lot of responsibility at home for cooking and cleaning because her parents work long hours in the fields. She has extended family with whom she spends time, and she often serves as a caretaker for her younger cousins. Her family has strong ties to Mexico and goes there each year in December and April, staying a month each time.

Far from being a troublemaker, Teresa has gone through school as an extremely quiet and shy student. The only time that she is vocal and outgoing is when she is playing soccer or showing her karate skills. Teresa was so shy when she entered Grace's classroom that she would only talk in groups of other Latina girls, preferably her personal friends. If any boys or unknown students were in her group, she would not talk.

Part of the eighth-grade requirement for language arts is for students to make a presentation to the class. Teresa was very upset with this idea, and spoke to Grace privately about it several times, in tears. Because Teresa realized she struggled with reading and writing, she was even more reluctant to participate in the language arts class. Through Grace's support and many meaningful reading and writing activities, Teresa made progress during her eighth-grade year. She did do her class presentation during a unit on *el Día de los Muertos*.

Teresa is another type of LTEL student. She has been in schools in the United States and learned how to quietly remain unnoticed. Her frequent trips to Mexico probably also contributed to the fact that she was ignored. Her absences may have caused some of Teresa's academic problems, giving her some of the characteristics of a limited-formal-schooling student. Because she was quiet and turned in assignments, she was allowed to move from grade to grade. She may have received some ESL or bilingual support in early grades, but she arrived at junior high without literacy in either Spanish or English.

Characteristics of Older Struggling English Learners

As we read about the lives of these students, it is easy to become overwhelmed. Their personal and academic needs are far greater than those of their mainstream peers. Most teachers, even those with a background in working with English learners, are not prepared to work with these struggling older second-language students. Long-term English learners and recent im-migrants with limited formal schooling share certain characteristics (Schifini 1997; Short 1997; Yankay 1997). These students

♦ are overage for their grade-level placement due to their weak academic skills and limited or inadequate formal schooling

♦ have needs that traditional ESL and bilingual programs, and regular programs for native English speakers, cannot or do not meet

♦ have no or low literacy skills in their first language or in English, and have little academic content-area knowledge

♦ are socially and psychologically isolated from mainstream students

♦ need approaches and materials that will help them catch up to and compete with mainstream students

♦ are at risk of failing or dropping out in traditional academic programs

These two groups of struggling English learners also differ in significant ways. To work effectively with all their students, teachers must be aware of both the similarities and the differences. In Chapter 1, we discussed a socio-cultural difference between the two groups. Many limited-formal-schooling students have the characteristics of immigrant minorities, while many long-term English learners are more like involuntary minorities. As a result, teachers of LTELs need to plan activities that will help their students value their own cultural heritage and value school.

One similarity the two groups share is the need to develop academic English. The following sections discuss the differences between conversational and academic language proficiency, a distinction that has important implications for teaching both types of older English learners.

Conversational and Academic Language Proficiency

Based on the research of Skutnabb-Kangas (1979) with Finnish students in Sweden and on his own research with immigrant students in Canada, Cummins (1981) observed that many teachers, administrators, and school psychologists assumed that children had overcome all difficulties with their new language when they could converse easily in the language. Because these same students struggled with academic tasks, they were often assigned to special education classes or labeled as being lazy or unmotivated.

His research led Cummins to develop a distinction between basic interpersonal communicative skills (BICS), or conversational language, and cognitive academic language proficiency (CALP)—academic language. He found that it takes longer for English learners to develop academic language in English than to gain conversational language proficiency:

> Conversational aspects of proficiency reached peer-appropriate levels usually within about two years of exposure to L2 [a second language] but a period of five to seven years was required, on average, for immigrant students to approach grade norms in academic aspects of English. (Cummins 2000, 58)

Research by Collier (1989, 1992) and others has supported Cummins' early findings. Students need about two years to develop conversational language, but academic language takes at least twice as long to develop.

According to Cummins, conversational language is both context-embedded and cognitively undemanding. Language is context-embedded when there are many nonlinguistic clues present to make the meaning clear. In a conversation, we get clues from the gestures and intonation the speaker uses. We also get clues if the speaker points to objects or people around us. All these clues help provide a context for the language.

Teachers of English learners enrich the linguistic context for their students by using pictures, gestures, intonation, and other nonlinguistic cues. These are external cues that make the English input more comprehensible. Krashen (1982) has argued that comprehensible input is what leads to language acquisition. Teachers can also enrich the context by drawing on students' interests and background knowledge. As Cummins points out, "contextual support involves both internal and external dimensions. Internal factors are attributes of the individual that make a task more familiar or easier in some respect" (2000, 72).

Conversational language is also cognitively undemanding. Cognitive demand might be thought of as the amount of mental energy it takes to discuss a topic or complete a task. When students discuss topics that are familiar and culturally relevant, the language is cognitively undemanding. Basic interpersonal communicative skills come into play when two people talk face-to-face about the weather or the success of a local sports team.

Academic language, in contrast, is both context-reduced and cognitively demanding. Reading a social studies text involves using academic language. The only clues for the reader come from the text itself. Often, the pictures, charts, and graphs do not help English learners make sense of the text, so the language of the book is context-reduced. If the text deals with challenging new concepts, then it is cognitively demanding.

Cummins has explained that the difference between conversational and academic language is not the same as the difference between oral and written language. Reading a picture postcard from a friend could be an instance of conversational language, while listening to an academic lecture would require the use of academic language. The distinction between the two is really a difference in register. As Cummins puts it,

> Oral classroom discussions do not involve reading and writing directly, but they do reflect the degree of students' access to and command of literate or academic registers of language. This is why CALP [cognitive, academic language proficiency] can be defined as expertise in understanding and using literacy-related aspects of language. (2000, 70)

Two features of academic language registers are *vocabulary* and *syntax*. Academic vocabulary is more specialized and often has Latin or Greek roots rather than Anglo-Saxon origins. Figure 2–1 lists some common Anglo-Saxon words, their French equivalents, and their Latin or Greek synonyms. Academic language contains many more words like those in the French and Latin/Greek columns than it does Anglo-Saxon words.

For Spanish speakers, even those with limited schooling, some Latinate words may be accessible because Spanish derives from Latin, and many common words in Spanish are scientific words in English. For example, Sandra's limited schooling students understand when she uses the word *difuncto* to mean a dead person during discussions about the *Día de los Muertos* (Day of the Dead), or the word *concluir* (to conclude), when they discuss science experiments and come to conclusions about their data collection. Teachers of native Spanish–speaking students can capitalize on students' familiarity with words like these, and in Chapter 4 we discuss in more detail how teachers can use cognates.

Vocabulary that is part of the academic register also includes familiar words with specialized meanings. For example, the word *fault* could be part

Common Anglo-Saxon Word	French Equivalent	Latin or Greek Synonym
ask	question	interrogate
dead	deceased	defunct
end	finish	conclude
fair	beautiful	attractive
fear	terror	trepidation
help	aid	assist
rise	mount	ascend
thin	spare	emaciated

FIGURE 2–1. *Roots of Academic English Words*

of a student's conversational language register. Many students understand the word in the expression "It's not my fault." The same students might not recognize the word in a geology text, in which *fault* takes on a specialized meaning.

Academic registers are characterized by sentences that contain two or more clauses. This more complex syntax poses a challenge for English learners. For example, in the sentence "Because he knew how to convert liquid into gas, the student volunteered to conduct the experiment," there are two clauses, and a reader has to comprehend the relationships among the ideas being presented. This is a cognitively demanding task. Unless the student has read many texts like this, it is also a context-reduced task.

To give you a better idea of academic language, read the following short paragraph from an introductory linguistics text:

> Some linguists understand the phoneme somewhat more concretely and view is as a representation of an ideal articulatory target. Because of the effects of the environment in which the phoneme occurs, however, it may be produced in different allophonic shapes. In any case, phonemic writing represents the basic, contrasting sound units of a language. (Akmajian, Demers, and Harnish 1984, 129)

This passage contains a number of technical words, such as *phoneme* and *allophonic,* as well as familiar words with specialized meanings, like *shape.* The syntax is complex. In the second sentence, for example, the main idea comes at the end, and the first part of the sentence gives the reason. The sentence may be seen as expressing cause and effect and also as showing a contrast, as signaled by *however.* The point here is simply that this kind of language is much more cognitively demanding and context-reduced than the language of typical conversations.

Goals for Instruction

TESOL, the professional organization for Teachers of English to Speakers of Other Languages, has published a book outlining goals and standards for school-age English learners (Kupetz 1997). There are three goals, and the first two correspond to the distinction between conversational language and academic language:

> **Goal 1: To use English to communicate in social settings**
> Standards for Goal 1
> > Students will:
> > 1. use English to participate in social interaction
> > 2. interact in, through, and with spoken and written English for personal expression and enjoyment
> > 3. use learning strategies to extend their communicative competence
>
> **Goal 2: To use English to achieve academically in all content areas**
> Standards for Goal 2
> > Students will:
> > 1. use English to interact in the classroom
> > 2. use English to obtain, process, construct, and provide subject matter information in spoken and written form
> > 3. use appropriate learning strategies to construct and apply academic knowledge (9)

Students who meet these two goals will have developed both conversational and academic language. The third goal is for students to use English in socially and culturally appropriate ways. The TESOL standards book contains clear explanations of the standards and useful vignettes of classrooms in which teachers use instructional practices to achieve the goals and meet the standards.

The Language Proficiency of Older English Learners

Long-term English learners have generally acquired conversational English. As a result, they are often placed in mainstream classes. If they do poorly in school, they may be recommended for special education classes, since the assumption is that difficulty with English is not the problem. Unfortunately, some LTELs have even lost conversational proficiency in their first language in the process of acquiring English.

However, some LTELs have not developed conversational English. Oscar's student Marisol, for example, spoke little English when Oscar started working with her. Whether or not LTELs speak conversational English depends a great deal on the contact they have had with English speakers. Schumann (1978) proposed that the social distance between immigrant groups and the mainstream helps account for their rate of language acquisition. Some LTELs have been quite isolated from native English speakers even though they have lived much of their life in the United States. Such students, though, are usually the exception.

Although they may have developed conversational language, LTELs face the task of developing academic language. They do not know how to talk, read, and write about school subjects in their first language or in English. In fact, teachers sometimes conclude that some English learners have *no* language. We would argue that they do have language—they just don't have the language that is appropriate for and valued in the school setting.

New arrivals, on the other hand, may speak little or no English even for conversational purposes, although some students with adequate formal schooling who have studied English in their native country may be at an advanced-beginner or low-intermediate level in their conversational English. Most new arrivals develop conversational language fairly quickly as they interact with English speakers both in and out of school, although older students may not gain native-like pronunciation.

It is easier for new arrivals who have developed academic proficiency in their first language to develop academic proficiency in English. They still need to develop the English vocabulary and syntax that characterize academic English, but they already have an implicit knowledge of how academic language works.

Most new arrivals with limited or interrupted formal schooling face an especially difficult challenge to developing academic English. There is a significant gap between their academic knowledge and skills and the knowledge and skills of many of their classmates. They must develop content knowledge and learn the academic registers of English needed to discuss concepts. They must do this in a short period of time because they are soon to enter high school; or, if they are already in high school, they will soon attempt to join the workforce or enter some form of higher education. For teachers of these students, closing the achievement gap is a real challenge.

Although long-term English learners and students with limited formal schooling generally differ in the area of conversational English, they are alike in that both lack academic English. Figure 2–2 shows the kinds of language proficiency each of the types of English learners has typically acquired.

Newly arrived students with adequate schooling have both conversational and academic proficiency in their first language. They may also have learned some conversational English. Alondra is one of the few of Sandra's newcomer students who arrived with literacy and academic proficiency in her first language. Alondra went to kindergarten and part of first grade in the United States, then went back to Mexico. She entered Sandra's class at

Type of English Learner:	Conversational Language		Academic Language	
	English	First Language	English	First Language
Newly arrived with adequate schooling	(X)	X	–	X
Newly arrived with limited formal schooling	–	X	–	–
Long-term English learner	(X)	X	–	–

(X) = only applies to some members of the group

FIGURE 2–2. *Language Proficiency Developed by Different Types of English Learners*

the end of her fifth-grade year. Sandra explains that Alondra was well pre-pared when she arrived:

> In Mexico she did not miss school. She was almost on grade level in reading in Spanish when she came. We worked on writing conven-tions in Spanish together. She was very disciplined and determined to learn, so I gave her short novels in Spanish to read on her own time, and she did improve.

Although Alondra was extremely shy and quiet, her written work re-flected her previous schooling. During the study of Cinderella stories from around the world, Sandra's class wrote a language-experience "Mexican Cinderella" story together drawing on events they had read about in other Cinderella stories. Then the students responded in various ways. One thing they did was to list characters, setting, and key events in the story. When asked to list the events in the class story, Alondra wrote

> Se visitio con un vestido de fiesta y un huarache de vidrio que encon-tro envuelto en la "quilt" (cobija) de su mama.
>
> (Translation) She dressed up in a party dress and glass sandal that she found wrapped in her mother's quilt.

Although she does not use accents, Alondra's spelling is conventional. In fact, she even puts the silent *h* on the word *huarache* (sandal). Writing the silent *h* is a specific skill taught in school. In addition, Alondra uses sophis-ticated structures such as the participle *envuelto* (wrapped).

Alondra also makes connections between Spanish and her new lan-guage. The class had made quilts, and Alondra clarifies for the reader that the *cobija* is like a quilt. The last item in her listing of events gives us more information about her academic language proficiency:

> Se casaron y vivieron felieces en un rancho cercano.
>
> (Translation) They got married and lived happily on a nearby ranch.

Here Alondra uses language that is more literary than colloquial. She uses *felices* (although misspelled) for *happy*, a more literary word than *contento*, which is more commonly used in conversation. Another word she uses is *cercano* (nearby), a word most often found in literature.

In English, Alondra also uses an academic register. Students who have developed academic registers in their first language begin to use academic English fairly quickly even though their writing may still contain many errors typical of most second-language students. Alondra's introductory paragraph to a long summary she wrote for the class Mexican Cinderella story shows she knows how stories should begin (Figure 2–3). The details provide the necessary information and background. The writing gives evidence of her first-language literacy. She uses the word *indigenous* to describe the native people in the story, drawing on the Spanish cognate *los indígenas*. In fact, she even appears to have accented the English over the second *i*, showing she knows that word has an accent in her native language. She is transferring her knowledge of Spanish accents, a skill that students learn in Mexico. Alondra, then, is a newcomer who has academic language in Spanish and is beginning to transfer this to English. Figure 2–3 shows this introductory paragraph.

Students who have not developed the academic register of their first language take longer to develop academic English. Roberta is a long-term English learner who lacks academic language and concepts in English and Spanish. She speaks Spanish and quite a bit of English, but clearly understands and speaks her heritage language better.

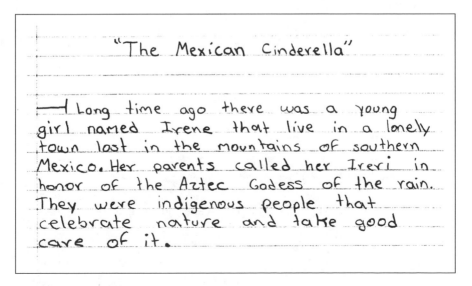

FIGURE 2–3. *Alondra's English Wring*

At eighteen Roberta has had nine years of schooling in the United States. She began in kindergarten but, because her family maintains strong ties with Mexico, she traveled often to Mexico for extended family visits. When Roberta was in her sophomore year in high school, she dropped out of school for two years to go to Mexico because her grandmother got very sick. After her grandmother died, she returned to the United States. Because of her missed schooling and her low grade point average (GPA) of .0929, she was placed back in the tenth grade in a continuation high school.

When Veronica, a research assistant and student at our university, was assigned to work with Roberta, she was concerned about her GPA and the limited academic course work she was receiving. Veronica interviewed Roberta using a student survey she developed with Yvonne (Figure 2–4).

Student Survey

Name_____ Grade_____

Appropriate grade_____ Age_____

Schooling background:

Language more comfortable in for

     Speaking_____

     Writing_____

Tell me something about yourself:

1. What do you like to do? What do you like about your friends?

2. Are you living with your family? Tell me about your family.

3. Are you working? Do you like your job? Would you like to learn more about that job? Are you in any kind of training program?

4. What are your career goals? What do you see yourself doing in five years?

5. What do you think you need to achieve those goals? How could you find out?

FIGURE 2–4. *Student Survey*

In school:

1. Who was/is your favorite teacher? Why?

2. What is or has been your favorite subject? Why?

3. How do you feel about yourself as a student?

4. What do you feel you are good at in school?

5. What do you feel you need the most help with in school?

6. Do you like to read? What do you read?

7. What do you think a good reader does when he or she reads?

8. How do you feel about your writing in English?

Language and culture:

1. What language do you speak at home? In school?

2. With whom do you speak English? Spanish?

3. Are you most comfortable in English? Spanish?

4. Can you read and write in Spanish?

5. How do you feel about your first language and culture?

FIGURE 2–4. *Student Survey (continued)*

Veronica used either English or Spanish when conducting the survey, depending on the student's language proficiency.

Veronica also collected writing samples from Roberta to assess her academic proficiency in both her first and second languages. Veronica found that Roberta spoke Spanish very well and was most comfortable using Spanish, though she spoke English with friends and teachers. Her writing samples also revealed that her writing in Spanish was stronger than her writing in English. Her Spanish response in Figure 2–5 shows some spelling errors in

Lo que no me gusta de la escuela.
No me gusta lavantarme muy tamprano
an la manaña. Otra cosa que no me
gusta as las mathimaticas. Me gusta muy
poqueito. Otra cosa que no me gusta
as la comida. No me gusta porque todo
los dias dan lo misimo y me anfado.

FIGURE 2–5.   *Roberta's Writing in Spanish*

an academic word, *mathimaticas*, which should be *matemáticas*, as well as in colloquial words like *poqueito*, which should be *poquito*, and *misimo*, which should be *mismo*. Perhaps what is more telling is the way Roberta uses repetitious phrasing and colloquial vocabulary. Her writing in Spanish contains many features of conversational language rather than representing academic language.

Roberta's piece in English explaining what she likes about school (Figure 2–6) is perhaps even more telling. Her difficulty in expressing herself

What I most like about school.
The think I most like about
school, is the teachers. Most of the
teachers taaches ok. Another thing
I liha about school, is my business
class, bacausa you do racorad kaaping.
Although thing I liha about school
is P.E. bacausa you run and exsrcias.

FIGURE 2–6.   *Roberta's Writing in English*

in written English is obvious. She misspells or confuses common words (*thing* and *think*). Her style is repetitious. She uses "another thing" as her only transition. She translates literally from Spanish *Lo que me gusta de la escuela es:* "The *think* I most like about school is." This paragraph is quite brief. Roberta does write complex, cause-and-effect sentences using "because." However, her written language contains many features of conversational English. Although Roberta has developed conversational proficiency in two languages, her writing samples show that she lacks academic proficiency in both.

Using Preview/View/Review

Students like Alondra have already developed the academic register of their first language, and teachers can draw on this strength to help them learn academic English. Even students who have not developed the academic register of their first language, like Roberta, do have conversational proficiency in that language, and teachers can give them access to academic English and subject-matter concepts by the proper use of their first language.

An important strategy for drawing on students' first languages and teaching academic content is Preview/View/Review (Freeman and Freeman 1998, 2000). In this strategy, key concepts are introduced in the students' first languages (preview). Then students are given opportunities to work with those concepts in their new language, English (view). Teachers use a number of techniques to make the English instruction comprehensible, including hands-on activities, visuals, and *realia*. Finally, students are allowed to review the concepts in their first language to clarify, summarize, and ask questions.

If teachers do not speak their students' first languages, other students, classroom aides, or community members can be used to give the preview and review. If there are no resource people to help, students can be grouped by first languages, brainstorm on topics in their first languages, and report back to the teacher in English for both the preview and review portions of the lesson. Figure 2–7 shows how Preview/View/Review works. This strategy helps all English learners, whether they have developed academic proficiency in their first language or not.

Preview/View/Review		
Preview	first language	The teacher gives an overview of the lesson or activity in the students' first language (this could be giving an oral summary, reading a book, showing a film, asking a key question, etc.).
View	second or target language (English)	The teacher teaches the lesson or directs the activity in the students' second language.
Review	first language	The teacher or the students summarize key ideas and raise questions about the lesson in their first language.

FIGURE 2–7.   *Preview/View/Review*

Conclusion

In this chapter we described a number of students who fit into one of two categories: new arrivals with limited formal schooling and long-term English learners. Our hope is that these examples will help teachers as they think about their own students and the challenges those students face.

We also explained the difference between conversational and academic language. School success depends on the development of the academic register of the language of instruction. Students may appear to have proficiency in a language if they can follow classroom instructions or converse on everyday topics, but this conversational proficiency is not the same as the academic proficiency needed to succeed in school. Traditional ESL programs have often focused on helping students develop conversational English. Newer programs in which teachers teach language through academic content are aimed at helping students develop academic language. Teachers of struggling older English learners should make the development of academic language a priority. In the chapters that follow, we give examples of teachers who do just that.

Professional Extensions

1. Identify one student, in your classroom or the classroom of another teacher, who you believe has the characteristics of a limited-formal-schooling student. Identify one who has the characteristics of a long-term English learner.
2. Interview the two students you identified using the student survey shown in Figure 2–4 or using questions you develop on your own. Describe the students as we have in this chapter, giving their grade level, schooling background, and current personal and school situations.
3. Review the discussion of conversational and academic language proficiency. Identify a student who appears to have conversational proficiency but lacks academic proficiency. Interview that student using the student survey or your own interview sheet. Ask the student to write something for you. From the information you gather, analyze the student's conversational and academic proficiency.
4. Consider how you might use Preview/View/Review. Explain how you would implement it with your students or in a class that you have observed.

Research on Effective Practices for Older English Learners

Lo que no me gusta de la escuela

Lo que no me gusta de la escuela es lo dificil que es acomodarse entre los demas cuando no conoses a nadie. No me gusta porque lo que yo quisiera es tener las clases normales como todos los demas pero no puedo porque mi ingles es muy poquito.

(Translation) What I don't like about school is how difficult it is to be part of everything when you don't know anyone. I don't like it because I would like to have normal classes like the other students, but I can't because I have so little English.

This short piece was written by Francisca, the seventeen-year-old girl described in Chapter 2. She was writing for her college tutor, Veronica. Veronica used the student survey form depicted in Figure 2–4 and writing samples to get to know Francisca as she was tutoring her. The school had placed

Francisca in the ninth grade, and Veronica wanted to find out about her interests and her reading and writing ability. Although Francisca did not feel she could write in English, her sixth-grade education in Mexico allowed her to write to Veronica in Spanish and tell her how she felt about school. Her social isolation and her understanding that she was behind other students academically because of her lack of English comes across clearly in her writing.

Lack of self-confidence is common among English learners and is even more acute when they are placed at lower grade levels than would be normal for someone their age. Sandra tells about Yesica, a Trique speaker who was placed in Sandra's multiage newcomer class. Because Yesica lived in a remote part of southern Mexico and was needed to do chores at home, she was not sent to school at all until she was nine, a year before she moved to the United States. School officials in her village placed Yesica in first grade with six and seven year olds. Partly because of the structured schooling approach and partly because of her embarrassment at being so old in first grade, Yesica learned very little in her one year of schooling.

In Sandra's class Yesica's age was considered, and she was identified as a fifth grader. However, coming to school in this country with such limited previous schooling was very traumatic for her. Yesica did not know how to behave, and at first she responded with silence. Sandra describes Yesica at the beginning:

> She had to learn not only the language but she had to learn to be in school, sit still for many hours and interact with students of her same age. The task was not easy, and she struggled to become a member of our learning community. Her struggles were reflected in her rejection of students, silent periods (even during recess and lunch times) and reluctance to make friends. After 3 months she began to blossom.

Yesica's story is a positive one since she eventually became one of Sandra's best students. She is now in middle school and comes back to volunteer in Sandra's classroom during her vacation times. She also comes to Sandra for academic help from time to time. She worked hard with Sandra for two years, but she has not made up the entire schooling gap.

Not all students have the kind of positive experience Yesica had. Many have negative experiences that can hinder their academic progress. Often, struggling older English learners drop out. Paj, the Hmong student also described in Chapter 2, became completely alienated from school and even told the researchers working with her that "The teacher doesn't care, and I don't care." This hopelessness shows the magnitude of the challenges these students face. Unless the curriculum is appropriate and the teachers are supportive and knowledgeable, older English learners do not move toward either English proficiency or academic competence.

The Challenge of Enabling Older English Learners to Close the Achievement Gap

In a recent summary of research on developments in schools, G. García (2000) listed three key concerns for policy makers and school administrators:

♦ the growing number of students who arrive at school ill prepared to learn;

♦ the growing number of non-native (foreign) born children and youth who enroll in schools across all grade levels; and

♦ the large number of native and foreign-born students who are limited English proficient (LEP). (1)

Many students who enter upper-elementary, middle, and high schools have little or no prior formal schooling, like Yesica, or they are long-term English learners, like Francisca. A report from the Center for Applied Linguistics summarizes the challenges such students face:

> [Older English learners] must learn to read, write, understand, and speak English; develop academic literacy in English to make the transition to the labor force or into other educational programs; and become socialized into American society during adolescence, a time of major emotional, physical, and psychological change. (1998, 1)

How are schools doing? Are they helping older English learners to close the achievement gap? Some researchers have found a discrepancy between what is known to be effective instruction for these students and the actual practices being implemented in schools.

Both G. García (2000) and Hughes (2000), for example, note that because the students struggle, they are given basic skills and repetitive drills rather than activities to build the high-level content knowledge, language, and comprehension skills they need. Seldom do schools help these students build on what they know and have experienced. Further, such students often attend schools that have limited access to technology, or where the technology that is available is used to drill and teach basic, rather than higher-order, skills. Rarely do teachers engage these students in modeling and simulation exercises or in cooperative learning, approaches that have proven to be effective with English learners.

Berman (1992) conducted research showing that many schools have not implemented the kinds of programs that are effective for struggling older English learners. He reported that students are placed in a passive role, classes are organized as age-based groups in which there is tracking, and the curriculum is abstract and driven by college entrance requirements and standardized tests. The classroom climate is generally impersonal, with few connections between the curriculum and the students' lives.

Valdés (2001) has written a powerful, rich description of a two-year study she did of four newcomer Latino middle-school students and the teachers of those focal students. She interviewed the students, their parents, the teachers, and other school personnel and spent hours observing the students in their classrooms. Her conclusions support Berman's and Hughes' research concerning the tracking and ineffective instruction many English learners experience in schools. In the three periods of daily ESL instruction students in Valdés' study received, there were no opportunities for these beginning ESL students to interact with native English speakers.

> They were completely isolated from English-speaking same-age peers. All interactions in English took place exclusively with the teacher at a rate of 1 to 30 or 35. The rest of the time, they were engaged in seatwork focused on learning vocabulary or copying sentences. Little went on in the classroom that could prepare them to develop the kinds of proficiencies they would need to succeed in other classes. Teachers' goals and objectives involved following the textbook, teaching English-language forms, and sometimes merely keeping the children quiet. (147)

The kind of instruction the ESL students in Valdés' study received contrasts with the type of effective instruction Berman and Hughes found to be effective. They found that effective schools group students heterogeneously and engage them in meaningful activities. Students in those schools work within appropriate developmental groups on thematic and integrated curriculum. In effective schools, standards are redefined, with a focus on authentic outcomes and indicators. Administrators, teachers, and support personnel take an active interest in students and celebrate and embrace their strengths and diversity.

In his summary of research on the needs of language-minority students, Goldenberg (1996) critiques classrooms where students are given whole-class instruction and seat work with limited opportunities "to talk, ask and answer questions, read aloud, and otherwise actively engage in learning language and content" (354). He calls for programs that offer challenging content, and he encourages the use of students' first languages to ensure that challenging content is made comprehensible.

Cummins (2000) and others have attributed the discrepancy between what is known to be effective instruction for language-minority students and the education that many of them receive to the unequal distribution of power in U.S. society. Simply put, English learners generally come from social groups that lack the power to shape social institutions, such as schools, to accommodate their needs. Schools, like other social institutions, tend to maintain the status quo of social groups. However, some schools have implemented the kinds of transformative programs and practices that result in academic success for all students, including English learners.

Meeting the Challenge by Implementing Research-Based Practices

Schools that meet the challenge presented by older English learners follow practices that are consistent with research on effective schools, such as those suggested by García, Valdés, Berman, Hughes, and Goldenberg. Their research and our own observations led us to develop the keys for school success listed in Figure 1–2. This section shows parallels between our keys and the recommendations of other researchers.

Key 1: Engage Students in Challenging, Theme-Based Curriculum to Develop Academic Concepts

The U.S. Department of Education has issued a set of principles to guide state and local school districts in considering reform for the education of linguistically and culturally diverse students (George Washington University Center for Excellence 1996). These include having high expectations in both language and content; building on the previous experiences of students; taking their language and cultural backgrounds into consideration when assessing students; and being cognizant of the fact that the success of English learners is a responsibility shared by all educators, the family, and the community. When schools set high expectations and then provide programs that allow students to meet those expectations, schools demonstrate that they believe in students' potential.

In the same way, Moll (1988) explains that Latino students need "challenging, innovative, and intellectually rigorous curriculum" (467) that is meaningful and draws on their personal experiences. Moll is opposed to ability groups, which he says degrade students and show a lack of respect for them. Moll's research indicates that English learners thrive in classrooms where teachers are given autonomy and opportunities to reflect upon their teaching in order to better meet students' needs.

Teachers who believe in their students often become advocates for them. Moll (1994) identified three key characteristics of effective teachers working with English learners:

1. They were able to articulate theory and tell why they did what they did.
2. They were able to argue with administrators to allow them to select materials and implement curriculum according to their professional judgment.
3. They drew on support from colleagues who shared their approach to teaching.

These effective, knowledgeable teachers found ways to show both students and fellow educators that they believed in the potential of all the students they taught. They did this by implementing innovative student interactions including drama and cross-age tutoring, and providing multiple opportunities for students to develop oral and written language by drawing on first-language strengths. These practices enable students to develop their potential.

Hamayan (1994) looked at Southeast Asian refugee children who had not had formal literacy instruction and examined their exposure to environmental print as well as their familiarity with different forms and functions of literacy. She found that the limited-formal-schooling children she worked with lacked basic literacy concepts. They did not understand usual classroom writing activities, such as what to write in a daily journal. She concludes that

> because of the complexity of literacy development and the special characteristics of low-literacy children, various instructional approaches that provide meaningful and functional literacy activities while teaching the specific forms and structures of written language need to be part of the classroom environment. (298)

She goes on to list classroom characteristics that allow literacy to emerge naturally: providing meaningful environmental print, introducing activities centered on motivating literacy and constructing meaning, creating a low-anxiety environment, embedding instruction about forms and structures in meaningful activities, and integrating literacy instruction with academic content.

Gersten and Jiménez (1994) observed successful teachers during reading instruction. They looked particularly at ways teachers supported intermediate students who lacked first-language literacy and had difficulty reading in English. The researchers concluded that effective instruction for language-minority students challenges the students, encourages their involvement, provides them with opportunities for success, and includes scaffolding with a variety of graphic organizers to draw on their background knowledge and give them access to content. In addition, they found that effective teachers give frequent feedback, make the content comprehensible, encourage collaborative interactions, and show respect for cultural diversity. All these practices show a belief in student potential.

E. García (1999) has conducted research on attributes of effective teachers. One of his findings is that these teachers focus on meaningful instruction and organize curriculum around themes. He comments, "Students became 'experts' in thematic domains while also acquiring the requisite academic skills" (311). Teachers show a belief in student potential when they create conditions in which students can become "experts." Further, García reported on a special program for high school students that featured student-generated themes. As one teacher commented:

> Having student-generated themes formalized student input for curriculum [because] they create the theme, [and] we [teachers] let them imagine what they want to study. They write the curriculum at the start of the six-week unit. From assignment to assessment, they are more involved. (362)

This program was successful in part because teachers provided challenging curriculum by involving their students in choosing and developing the themes on which the curriculum was based.

Key 2: Draw on Students' Background—
Their Experiences, Cultures, and Languages

Our local school district in Fresno, California, provides a series of all-day inservices for all teachers. Teachers who attend are provided a substitute and given professional development credit. They can choose among sessions that feature the language, culture, and history of the primary immigrant groups in the district. Presenters include members of those groups. Often, students from the group that's being featured are brought in, and a moderator asks questions of student panels.

The Hmong people of Southeast Asia form a large proportion of the English learners in our district, so several of the inservice sessions highlight Hmong students. In this way, the district follows Vang's (2000) observation that preservice and inservice teacher training about Hmong culture helps teachers reach students more effectively. By letting teachers choose the sessions they wish to attend and giving them substitutes and professional development credit, the district encourages teachers to study the language and culture of their students.

Jiménez (2001) points out that the struggling Latino and Latina students he worked with thrived when their specific backgrounds and national origins were recognized and when the challenge they face at becoming competent bilinguals was acknowledged. In the school that Jiménez studied, Spanish-speaking students were not all lumped together and treated alike. Those who were not proficient in their native Spanish were not critiqued. Students from El Salvador or Guatemala were validated for their specific national origin, and students who served as language brokers for their monolingual Spanish-speaking relatives were given recognition. All the students were encouraged to connect their reading and writing in English to their own cultural backgrounds and to value the literacy of their communities, including the oral literacy traditions of storytelling. In these ways, educators at the school showed respect for the students' cultures, languages, and backgrounds.

Moran and colleagues (1993) explain that overage students (students who are older than their classmates) "thrive in environments where they are accepted, respected, made to feel that they belong, and given opportunities to be in charge of their own learning" (117). These students need teachers who build personal relationships with them and connect to their families. Moran et al. suggest several strategies for working with older English learners, including using students' first languages and background knowledge as a base for what they are learning.

It is especially important to show older students that they are accepted, and one way schools can do this is to validate their linguistic and cultural backgrounds. The reason Yesica struggled as an overage student in Mexico was that her native language and culture were not validated. In Sandra's class, Yesica's background was treated as an asset, not a liability.

Schifini (1997) has looked at struggling older immigrant students, including those with limited formal schooling. He makes specific suggestions for improving their literacy, including helping students feel part of the classroom community, drawing on students' background knowledge, and encouraging skill development through successful engagements with texts. A key is to build on what students bring to the classroom—their languages, cultures, and previous experiences—to help them develop the knowledge and skills they need to succeed academically.

Key 3: Organize Collaborative Activities and Scaffold Instruction to Build Students' Academic English Proficiency

Much of the research reported in the previous sections points to the need for student collaboration and scaffolded instruction. In addition, Chang (2001), whose research focused on struggling immigrant Asian-Pacific American students, calls for collaboration and scaffolding to help students build academic English proficiency.

Chang presents a checklist for effective teaching and for creating a positive learning environment for immigrant students. To create the checklist, she drew on standards for effective teaching developed by the Center for Research on Education, Diversity, and Excellence (CREDE) (see *<www.crede.ucsc.edu>*) and Gardner's (1983) theory of multiple intelligences. In particular, Chang developed Gardner's idea of diverse entry points in connection to immigrant students. Immigrant students have different strengths, interests, and backgrounds that can be drawn upon by sensitive, knowledgeable teachers as they teach. When teachers know their students, they can teach effectively by starting where the student is and moving the student to new understandings.

Chang suggests that teachers consider the following in planning lessons:

1. Joint Productive Activities: Students are encouraged to work with each other, the teacher, and parents to reach their instructional goals and objectives.
2. Language Development: Teachers provide students with opportunities to use conversational and academic language appropriately in a variety of settings, adjusting the language to students' experience with English and providing first-language support.
3. Contextualization: Teachers draw upon students' backgrounds and cultures and bring in guests who can foster respect for multicultural perspectives.
4. Challenging Activities: Teachers plan for and implement activities that encourage academic concept development by drawing on cultural funds of knowledge and using culturally appropriate approaches to teaching.
5. Instructional Conversations: Teachers organize their classrooms to ensure that conversation between the teacher and peers develops academic concepts and language.
6. Diverse Entry Points: In all content areas and in all interactive activities, the teacher is sensitive to the students' needs, interests, talents, and understandings and is able to use that information to extend students' learning.

Chang's checklist includes the first three keys for success that we have identified. She states that teachers need to provide challenging curriculum. She also points to the importance of building on students' culture, language, and background. In addition, she advocates the use of joint productive activities.

Key 4: Create Confident Students Who Value School and Value Themselves as Learners

Earlier we described Valdés' study of Latino middle school students (2001). Perhaps the most disturbing finding was how little access these students had to English speakers, meaningful curriculum, or opportunities that would lead them to academic success. All four students were mired in the ESL track. They found themselves in classes with other students whose

English was very limited. Their teachers did not show that they believed these students could succeed. As a result, they engaged them in many time-consuming activities, such as coloring pictures or playing a version of Hangman rather than in activities that would help them build academic concepts and language.

Even the two students who tried the hardest and were determined to succeed were confronted with constant barriers. They became discouraged and began to lose confidence in themselves as learners. The teachers were well intentioned, but they did not understand their students' needs or abilities. Valdés' study shows teachers that they must know their students and know how to give them access to academic content. The attitudes and curriculum the students encountered ultimately prevented them from valuing themselves as learners or valuing learning.

In their guide for educators and other advocates for immigrant students, Olsen and Jaramillo (1999) describe in detail how schools can institute changes that give immigrant students opportunities to build their confidence and come to value school. When schools implement these changes, older English learners can succeed and pursue further education. The changes involve professional development and advocacy, communication, and action. Olsen and Jaramillo point out that teachers and others working with immigrants must be involved in ongoing, sustained professional development that encourages both collaboration and individual reflection. Schools must have systems for analyzing data about student achievement and progress that go beyond looking at standardized test scores. Olsen and Jaramillo call for strong advocates at school sites who can meet together and implement needed changes in assessment and curriculum. They point out that educators need to understand the complexities of their students' lives and must learn from and listen to their English language learners in order to provide them with the opportunities they need to close the gap and achieve at high levels academically. Professional development for all school staff and special training for teachers and counselors is essential.

Often teachers feel overwhelmed by the needs of their students. Surveys of support staff working with overage English learners show that they need several types of support to help their students build self-confidence and academic competence:

♦ professional development workshops on relevant topics specific to this population

♦ curriculum development to produce instructional resources geared to meet the instructional needs of students

♦ intervisitation among programs and replication of promising practices

♦ policy and guideline development

♦ networking (Paiewonsky 1997, 17)

In schools and districts where these supports are provided, students have begun to close the achievement gap.

O. García (1999) studied limited-formal-schooling Latino high school students in the New York school system and found that the students' lives and backgrounds were extremely complex. She concluded that most educational programs designed to help these students "only act as a Band-Aid for a year" (79). She suggests alternative high school programs that would meet the needs of these students and provide the kinds of opportunities that Olsen and Jaramillo recommend. These alternative schools would have four features:

1. Literacy development in Spanish and English to help students gain social and scientific knowledge.
2. Nontraditional organization of students so they could work in small groups with one teacher providing most of the instruction.
3. Allowance for students to take longer than the traditional four years to earn the high school credits needed for graduation.
4. Flexible daily schedules so that students could work and attend school.

All four suggestions respond to student needs. Students in alternative high schools with these features would come to value school and to value themselves as learners.

Walsh (1991) provides guidelines to help school leaders develop programs that give all students opportunities to succeed. In order to help older struggling English learners meet academic challenges, school administrators must provide leadership in the development of appropriate programs. They must be knowledgeable about recent research and practices in bilingual and ESL education for older students, and must put into place programs that meet these students' special needs. The programs should be flexible and ungraded to allow students to move at their own pace. Classes should be small, and literacy and content should be taught thematically. In addition, placement and exit criteria should be well-defined.

Walqui (2000) studied a successful academic program for immigrant students at Calexico High School in California. Based on her observations, she lists ten characteristics of schools that provide all students with opportunities to become confident, competent learners. In such schools:

1. The culture of the classroom fosters the development of a community of learners, and all students are part of that community.
2. Good language teaching involves conceptual academic development.
3. Students' experiential backgrounds provide a point of departure and an anchor in the exploration of new ideas.
4. Teaching and learning focus on substantive ideas that are organized around themes with concepts presented cyclically.
5. New ideas and tasks are contextualized.
6. Academic strategies, sociocultural expectations, and academic norms are taught explicitly.
7. Tasks are relevant, meaningful, engaging, and varied.
8. Complex and flexible forms of collaboration maximize learners' opportunities to interact while making sense of language and content.
9. Students are given multiple opportunities to extend their understandings and apply their knowledge.
10. Authentic assessment is an integral part of teaching and learning. (1–2)

The four keys for school success we have presented in this chapter are interrelated. In schools where teachers provide challenging curriculum; build on students' backgrounds, languages, and cultures; and organize collaborative, scaffolded instruction to help students build academic English proficiency, the students become more confident. They begin to value themselves as learners and to value school. In the process, they start to close the gap between their current proficiency level and the level schools expect for students their age.

In their research with over seven hundred thousand language-minority students in five large urban and suburban public school districts in various regions of the United States, Thomas and Collier (1997) identify the three most important predictors of academic success, which are consistent with our four keys. Thomas and Collier found that these predictors were more important than background variables such as poverty or inadequate preparation, which have in the past spelled academic failure. Below we summarize those three predictors:

1. Using cognitively complex academic instruction in students' first languages for as long as possible as well as in the target language.
2. Using current approaches to teaching, including cooperative learning groups studying thematic units to teach the academic curriculum through two languages.
3. Changing the sociocultural contexts of schools to value students' cultures and languages and to create a warm, safe, supportive learning environment.

Teaching Language Through Content Organized Around Themes

Older English learners who struggle academically are always facing the battle of time. They need to become proficient users of English and catch up academically to their age-level peers. Their peers have learned language and subject-matter content at the pace that schools expect, but these older learners have missed years of schooling or fallen behind their peers academically. They need to develop academic content knowledge and proficiency in the academic register of English. And they have limited time to close the achievement gap.

Collier (1995) points out that school success depends on students' developing cognitive, academic, and language proficiency. These three areas are interrelated. Cognitive development results from solving problems in or out of school. Academic development involves problem solving during content-area studies. Linguistic development enables students to use academic language to engage in these problem-solving activities and achieve academically.

The best way to help students learn both English and school subjects is to teach language through content that is organized thematically. We have explained three reasons for teaching language through content (Freeman and Freeman 1998a):

1. Students get *both* language and content. Research has shown that students can learn English and subject-matter content material at the same

time. Students don't need to delay the study of science or literature until they reach high levels of English. Instead, they can learn both simultaneously. Given the time limitations older students face, it is crucial that classes provide them with both academic content-area knowledge and academic English.

2. Language is kept in its natural context. When teachers teach science in English, students learn science terms as they study biology or chemistry. The vocabulary occurs naturally as students read and discuss science texts.

3. Students have reasons to use language for real purposes. The primary purpose of school is to help students develop knowledge of different academic disciplines. When academic content is presented in English, students focus on the main purpose of schooling: learning science, math, social studies, or literature. In the process, they also learn English.

Content-based language instruction is most effective when the content is organized around themes. The first key for success is to develop challenging, theme-based curriculum. In the successful high school program García (1999) reported on, the curriculum was based on student-generated themes. Similarly, Marsh (1995) describes a dual-language program for high school students in which students studied content through themes. The program included many students from the Dominican Republic. One project involved students in New York City and Santo Domingo. Groups of students chose to investigate specific aspects of the two places, including the geography, agriculture, topography, and architecture. They learned social studies content as they compared and contrasted various aspects of the two areas.

Content-based language instruction differs from traditional approaches for second-language students. Traditional approaches focus on aspects of the language itself (grammar and vocabulary) or on the social and cultural characteristics of the target-language group: English learners study sentence structure and vocabulary or the customs of English speakers.

As teachers move away from traditional approaches and begin to teach language through meaningful content, they must still be aware that their students are English learners. For that reason, teachers must find ways to make English instruction understandable. They can do this by enriching the linguistic context while at the same time presenting cognitively demanding content.

Strategies for Making Language and Content Understandable
If at all possible, preview and review the content in the students' first language.
1. Use visuals and realia (real things). Try always to move from the concrete to the abstract.
2. Use gestures and body language.
3. Speak clearly and pause often.
4. Say the same thing in different ways.
5. Write key words and ideas down. (This slows down the language for English language learners.)
6. Use overheads and charts whenever appropriate.
7. Make frequent comprehension checks.
8. Have students explain main concepts to one another working in pairs or small groups. They can do this in their first language.
9. Above all, keep oral presentations or reading assignments short. Cooperative activities are more effective than lectures or assigned readings.

FIGURE 3–1. *Strategies for Making Language and Content Understandable*

A number of strategies can help make English instruction comprehensible. Figure 3–1 lists several useful practices. (We elaborate on these in Chapter 5, in which we discuss strategies that effective teachers use.)

Stages of Language Acquisition

When students receive understandable messages—comprehensible input—in English, they begin to acquire the language. Krashen (1982) theorizes that people can acquire language when they receive input that is slightly beyond their current level of proficiency, provided that they are motivated to learn and not too apprehensive about learning. They can also use rules about the language to check their oral or written output. Knowing the rule for using quotation marks, for example, can help a student punctuate his or her writing. But it is comprehensible input that builds the basic proficiency that students need. If the input contains academic language, students will acquire the language needed for school.

As students acquire a new language, they go through a series of stages. Krashen and Terrell (1983) identified five stages that students pass through as they acquire a new language. Figure 3–2 lists the characteristics of each stage. It is important to recognize that students will go through these stages

Stages of Language Acquisition	
1 Preproduction	• Students produce little or no English. • Lessons focus on listening comprehension. • Lessons build receptive vocabulary.
2 Early Production	• Students respond with one- or two-word phrases. • Lessons expand receptive vocabulary. • Activities encourage students to produce vocabulary they already understand.
3 Speech Emergence	• Students respond in sentences. • Teachers model correct language forms. • Lessons continue to develop receptive vocabulary.
4 Intermediate Fluency	• Students engage in conversation and produce connected narrative. • Teachers model correct language forms.
5 Advanced	• Students refine their ability to use oral and written English that more nearly approximates the language of native speakers.

FIGURE 3–2. *Stages of Language Acquisition (based on Krashen and Terrell [1983])*

naturally and that their receptive language ability will exceed their productive ability. They will understand more than they can say or write, and teachers should continue to provide the comprehensible input they need for acquisition, even if the students are not speaking English.

As students acquire a new language, the teacher's responsibility is to make the input comprehensible and to use appropriate methods to assess students' progress. Even at the early stages of language acquisition, in which students produce little English, teachers can use a variety of strategies for checking comprehension. Figure 3–3 lists the kinds of oral and written responses that students at each stage can be expected to produce.

	Oral	Written
1 Preproduction	Students communicate with gestures, actions, yes/no answers, and names.	Students draw a picture or dictate a response that the teacher writes.
2 Early Production	Students respond to either/or questions using words or short phrases.	Students copy environmental print, label drawings, or write a simple message.
3 Speech Emergence	Students respond in longer phrases and sentences.	Given a graphic organizer, students write phrases or sentences.
4 Intermediate Fluency	Students engage in conversation and produce connected narrative.	Given a graphic organizer, students produce a narrative with a beginning, middle, and end.
5 Advanced	Students refine and extend oral ability.	Given a graphic organizer, students write several paragraphs with cohesive structure and connected sentences.

FIGURE 3–3.   *Student Responses for Varying Proficiency Levels*

ELD and SDAIE Classes

English learners will acquire English, moving through a series of natural stages, as they receive comprehensible input. As long as the input contains academic language and concepts, they will acquire the kind of language they need for school success. However, it is helpful to differentiate between content-based language instruction at earlier and later stages.

When students are just beginning to acquire English, they are not able to learn content-area subjects at the same rate or to the same depth as more advanced English learners can. For students in the early stages of English development, the focus is more on the acquisition of academic English than on gaining a thorough understanding of academic content. At more advanced stages of English proficiency, the focus shifts from language to content, and students can be expected to learn grade-level-appropriate academic subject matter.

The difference between the early and later stages has been recognized in many schools. Beginning students are placed in English language development (ELD) classes. Students in these classes are at early stages of English language development, and they may or may not have developed literacy or studied academic content in their first language. ELD classes focus on language development, and students are assessed for their language gains.

Courses for students at higher levels of English are classified as SDAIE (Specially Designed Academic Instruction in English). Students in SDAIE social studies or science classes are at the intermediate fluency or advanced stages of English acquisition, and they have literacy and grade-level-appropriate content knowledge in academic subjects in their first language. The focus is on content, and students are assessed for content even though teachers expect that their responses may not always show that all the conventions of English have been acquired.

Some older struggling English learners will move from ELD to SDAIE classes without developing primary language literacy. For example, some long-term English learners may have lost most of their primary language, and instruction in that language would not be comprehensible for them. It is possible for these students to develop background academic concepts and adequate levels of literacy entirely through study in a new language when teachers apply appropriate strategies. The task is not an easy one, but all students can move from ELD to SDAIE classes and eventually into the mainstream. It is important to use measures of literacy development and academic language to determine whether students are ready for more advanced classes, rather than relying solely on their conversational proficiency in English.

The differences between ELD and SDAIE classes are shown in Figure 3–4. An effective school program for English learners includes placement in the appropriate type and level of ELD or SDAIE class and careful monitoring of students as they increase their English proficiency. Eventually, students transition into mainstream classes.

We observed effective teaching in SDAIE classes when we worked with the Sunnyside School District in Tucson, Arizona (Freeman and Freeman 1998a). District administrators developed a special summer program that targeted high school students who had failed at least three of their classes the year before. Although all of the students spoke English, it was not their first language. Most had never learned to read or write in their primary language, so the instruction was in English. These students were long-term

	ELD (Most often used in elementary or secondary schools)	SDAIE (Most often used in middle schools and high schools)
Student Characteristics:	• English proficiency—beginner • First-language academic proficiency—not considered	• English proficiency intermediate to advanced • First-language academic proficiency—at grade level
Focus of Instruction and Evaluation:	• Language taught through content, with emphasis on language development • Evaluation focuses on language	• Grade-appropriate content taught using special techniques to make the language understandable • Evaluation focuses on academic content

FIGURE 3–4. *ELD and SDAIE*

English learners who lacked the academic language proficiency they needed to succeed.

In this special program, ESL teachers teamed with content-area teachers who were teaching U.S. history and biology, two courses required for graduation. The history teacher and his partner taught a unit on the American Revolution, bringing in current newspaper articles about revolutions to use for discussing the causes of revolution, reading short stories about the American Revolution to make the characters and events come alive, and watching films about the war to provide background. Students worked in groups using what they had learned and their social studies texts to decide what the major causes of the American Revolution were, what events and people were important to the outcome, and how the American Revolution could be compared to the other revolutions they had discussed in class. The readings and discussions helped make the academic content accessible to the students.

In the biology class, the teachers worked to help their students become curious about biology. They engaged the students in hands-on activities, including having them cut up fruits and vegetables and keep careful records of what they observed and learned. Through cooperative groups, sharing, and guided discussion, the students became more observant and began to use the academic language and concepts of biology.

The students in this special program passed both U.S. history and biology, which they had previously failed, because the teachers had adapted their teaching strategies to make the academic language of the class accessible to the students.

Conclusion

We have reviewed the research on effective instruction for older struggling English learners. There seems to be consensus among researchers on the components of an effective program. Our own research confirms the findings we report in this chapter. In the classrooms we have observed, effective teachers use practices that follow the four keys for success. By implementing practices that follow the four keys, these teachers afford all their students opportunities to close the achievement gap.

Professional Extensions

1. The research shows that older struggling English learners need engaging and challenging curriculum that helps them build academic language proficiency. They should be given opportunities to interact with others and use their background knowledge and experiences, and they should come to value themselves as learners. Identify an older limited-schooling student or a long-term English learner and look at the kinds of curriculum that student is receiving. Is it consistent with the research?

2. Jiménez talked about his concern that all Hispanic students are considered to be the same. Many teachers seem to think that all Spanish speakers have similar backgrounds and cultures. What are the different Hispanic cultures represented within the student population in your community? How do they differ? List some specific differences.

3. Walqui lists ten characteristics of effective schools for older English language learners. Which of the characteristics does your local school have?

4. Figure 3–1 lists some strategies for making language and content comprehensible. Describe a lesson that you have taught or observed. Which of the strategies were used?

5. Figure 3–3 suggests appropriate oral and written responses for students at different stages of language acquisition. List some specific activities organized around a theme or a big question that would be suitable for students at each of the five stages.

6. Does your local school or district distinguish between students who need ELD and those who are ready for SDAIE? Explain. How does your school identify and place students in course work?

Using Themes to Develop Academic Language and Content Knowledge

I teach the immigrant unit at the beginning of the year because I want us all to talk about our own experiences as immigrants in this country. I start by sharing my own story and everybody has a chance to share personal stories. This fosters our classroom community. Students connect with each other and they feel that even the teacher has gone through the same struggles they have as immigrants. It really makes our learning community stronger.

This quotation from Sandra shows that she has an understanding of and appreciation for her students and the importance of community. Sandra's teaching is intentional. She is constantly developing the cognitive, academic, and linguistic abilities of her students as she follows the research-based practices we discussed in the previous chapter. She engages students in challenging, theme-based activities to develop academic concepts. She draws on their background experiences, their cultures, and their languages. She organizes collaborative activities and scaffolds instruction to build their academic English proficiency. In Sandra's classroom, students begin to close the achievement gap as they come to value school and value themselves as learners (Freeman, Mercuri, and Freeman 2001).

The first key to success (Figure 1–2) is to engage students in challenging, theme-based activities to develop academic concepts. Sandra organizes all her curriculum around interwoven themes. This approach has been especially helpful for her students because they can make better sense of instruction in English when they study the content areas of math, science, social studies, and literature if they know what the major, theme-related topic is. They also pick up vocabulary that is repeated naturally within the theme. Because Sandra makes sure that the big questions for her themes are relevant to her students' lives, they find the curriculum interesting. Since they can follow the interesting content and are learning the vocabulary, her English learners are engaged and successful. Finally, because Sandra's themes deal with universal topics, all her students can be involved as she adjusts activities to the various levels of English language proficiency and the academic backgrounds of her students. Figure 4–1 lists the reasons for organizing curriculum around themes based on big questions.

1. Students see the big picture so they can make sense of English language instruction.
2. Content areas (math, science, social studies, literature) are interrelated.
3. Vocabulary is repeated naturally as it appears in different content-area studies.
4. Through themes based on big questions, teachers can connect curriculum to students' lives. This makes curriculum more interesting.
5. Because the curriculum makes sense, English language learners are more fully engaged and experience more success.
6. Because themes deal with universal human topics, all students can be involved, and lessons and activities can be adjusted to different levels of English-language proficiency.

FIGURE 4–1. *Reasons to Organize Around Themes*

In the last chapter we discussed the research base for using themes with English learners. In this chapter we describe in detail a theme study that Sandra uses in her fourth-, fifth-, and sixth-grade newcomer class. Next, we discuss the kinds of concepts students need to develop in school, and consider how concepts learned in one language transfer to a second language. We then briefly tell about other theme studies developed by teachers in upper-elementary, junior high, and high school. Finally, we describe some whole-school theme-based projects at the secondary level that were created when groups of teachers and researchers worked together.

Sandra's Immigrant Theme Study

Sandra begins her year with a theme study on immigrants because her newcomer students are themselves recent immigrants. Her students feel marginalized in their school because they are different, and even other Spanish-speaking students at the school tease them or ignore them because they do not speak English. Most of her students also have limited formal schooling, and many of them do not understand school routines or see themselves as successful learners. Sandra wants her students to value their roots and their experiences and to begin to build confidence in themselves as learners, so her big question for the theme study is "How do I fit in as an immigrant?" Sandra explains how the topic helps her students:

> Talking about the issues involved in being an immigrant makes my students feel comfortable in the classroom. It helps them to feel that they are not alone. A lot of people through the years have been immigrants in this country in different situations.

Immigrant Stories

The first thing Sandra does is talk with her students about why people come to this country. She writes on the board, "How did my family come to this country?" This question allows her students to consider not only how they arrived, but also how some of their relatives got here. After discussing this question with the whole class, the students take home an interview sheet with a series of questions they can ask their families (Figure 4–2). The questions are designed to elicit family members' stories about coming to America.

Entrevista para historias de inmigración Immigrant Stories Interview
Entrevista a cualquiera de los miembros de tu familia que haya pasado por esta experiencia. Trata de lograr muchos detalles en tu entrevista y de usar palabras descriptivas en la escritura. Interview any family member who has had an immigrant experience. Try to get as many details as possible from your interview and use those descriptive words in your writing.
1. *¿Cómo viniste tú o tu familia a este país?* How did you or your family come to this country?
2. *Describe en que vinieron y los obstáculos que tuvieron que pasar para llegar.* Describe how you came (by boat, car, or bus; on foot) and the obstacles you had to overcome to get here.
3. *¿Cómo te sentías antes de partir? ¿durante la travesía?* y *¿después de haberlo logrado?* How did you feel before leaving, during the trip, and after having succeeded in getting here?

FIGURE 4–2. *Immigrant Family Stories Interview*

The next day the students share their findings. Most of Sandra's students have never thought about the various reasons others have come here or how they got here, so as the students share their family stories, the class fills out a chart that lists why people come to the United States. Then the students write, as best they can in Spanish or in English, their own story or the story of a relative, relating it as an adventure.

Sandra expands their thinking about why immigrants come to a new country by reading several immigrant stories, including *Grandfather's Journey* (Say 1993) and *How Many Days to America* (Bunting 1988). Although some of her Mixteco and Trique students from southern Mexico might connect to the idea of escaping government oppression, which the Bunting book describes, the idea of coming to America for adventure and to learn more about the world, as *Grandfather's Journey* depicts, is completely new to them. Books like *Who Belongs Here?* (Knight 1993) and *Trip to Freedom*

(Nguyen and Abello 1997), which is also available in Spanish as *Nuestro viaje hacia la libertad*, reinforce students' knowledge about the struggles of those who come to this country for various reasons, including freedom from the fear of being killed in war.

When a book is also available in Spanish, Sandra sometimes reads the story in Spanish one day, then comes back to it in English later in the unit. Since students come to Sandra's classroom with various levels of English proficiency, this preview for her Spanish speakers in their first language gives some of them some access to the English text. For others, the second reading offers a chance to build a more complete understanding. So, for example, Sandra read *La journada de abuelo* to her students before reading *Grandfather's Journey*.

Comparison Activities

Sandra ties all the activities for her theme to literature because she recognizes the importance of helping her students develop high levels of literacy. She also wants to be sure that they are constantly building concepts and making conceptual connections. For example, in the story *Dear Abuelita* ("Dear Grandmother") (Keane 1997), which is also available in Spanish as *Querida abuelita*, the main character is a young boy writing to his grandmother comparing his new life as an immigrant in the city in the United States to his rural life in Mexico. For the boy, the language, the sounds, the school, the food, and even the sky at night are different.

As one of their first activities, Sandra has her students complete an art project with black construction paper and chalk, comparing the night sky in the country to the night lights of the buildings in their town. This hands-on activity helps them feel comfortable in the classroom as well as to express some of their feelings about being in a new and different place. The students then write letters to their relatives in Mexico, doing as the boy in the book did.

Quilt Making

Two other books that Sandra uses early in the year are *The Keeping Quilt* (Polacco 1988) and *The Tortilla Quilt* (Tenorio-Coscarelli 1996). Both of these books show the importance of remembering important life events. After reading them, Sandra and the students talk about memories they have of their families and their homelands. She then ties math and art into the reading:

I also do some math instruction connected to the books we read. I teach patterns. I show the students different pictures of quilts, and then as a group we compare the different patterns. We discuss what patterns are and talk about patterns in math. We use manipulatives to get the idea, and then the students start a project where they create a patterned quilt with different shapes and colors of construction paper. In the white slots the students can write memories of their families, friends, and country. This is a very powerful activity, and I use it to help my new arrivals to share some of the emotions they are feeling.

Class Immigrant Story

Sandra's routine includes a twenty- to forty-minute writing time each day. Because so many of her students have had limited reading and writing experience, Sandra needs to find ways to support their emerging literacy and to get them involved in the writing process. After the class has read and discussed several immigrant books and charted their own and other immigrants' experiences, Sandra puts students into heterogeneous groups, including in each group students who have strengths in art, in writing, or in understanding concepts (such as geography concepts). She gives the students a form to use as they brainstorm together about what their group's immigrant story will include. They must think of a title, a setting, some characters, the main events, and a conclusion. Once they have brainstormed, each group writes a story together. Figure 4–3 shows the graphic organizer Sandra gives the students to help them create their story.

Title
Characters
Setting
Events
Ending

FIGURE 4–3. *Immigrant Story Graphic Organizer*

The entire class comes together, and each group shares its main ideas. Next, the whole class votes on which ideas they want to use, then they compose a whole-class story as a language-experience activity. Sandra writes the story on an overhead transparency as students call out ideas. Students often contribute in Spanish, so Sandra is constantly asking the class, "How could we say that in English?" Students copy the story as Sandra writes it out. The length of this daily writing time varies. Sandra ends it when she sees that the students are tiring or losing interest for the day. This first story usually takes about six weeks to complete. When it's finished, the students illustrate it, bind it, and take it home to share with their families. One year the students made a play of their story and acted it out for some younger students at the school.

Geography and Social Studies

Sandra constantly weaves geography lessons with a multicultural emphasis into the theme study to expand her students' worldview. She and the students read *Scholastic News*. One issue had an article about the many different Hispanic groups living in the United States. This article really fascinated her students:

> We discussed the idea of other groups of Hispanics living here. Some of my students were amazed that, first of all, there was such a large number and then that there was such a long list of countries that Hispanics come from. It was a surprise to them to see the large number of immigrants who struggle just like they do. For most of my students, their world starts and ends with Mexico. It was a real eye-opener.

Sandra also has her students use maps and globes to look up all the countries that Hispanics come from. They choose several of the countries to research on the Internet.

To help her students develop math concepts, Sandra has the class do a bar graph. The students first graph their individual answers to the question "What time do you go to sleep at night?" Once students connect the bar graph concept to their own lives, the class works together on a large piece of butcher paper to make a bar graph showing the countries that Hispanics come from and how many come to the United States from each country. Of course, this involves the idea of grouping by thousands, another concept new to most of her students.

Sandra also reinforces the idea of diversity among immigrants through literature. Students read poetry from different sources, including *A Chorus of Cultures: Developing Literacy Through Multicultural Poetry* (Ada, Harris, and Hopkins 1993) and *I Am of Two Places* (Carden and Cappellini 1997) and its Spanish version, *Soy de dos lugares*. These books include poems written by immigrant children. Sandra also uses *Judge for a Day* (in Spanish as *Juez por un dia*) (Gonzalez-Jensen 1997), a patterned book that tells of a boy trying foods from all over the Spanish-speaking world. This story reinforces for her students the concept that Hispanics come from many different countries and have different customs and ways of looking at the world.

To help her students develop social studies concepts, Sandra puts up a wall chart that contains a map of the world and lists countries from which people have migrated to the United States. It also shows the century when most of the immigrants from each country arrived. Arrows connect each country listed to the correct part of the map. For example, an arrow from Africa identifies the Congo, Angola, Gambia, Nigeria, and Senegal as parts of Africa from which large numbers of immigrants have come. Many immigrants came from Nigeria in the 1500s and from the Congo and Angola during the 1600s. Using this wall chart as a model, Sandra's students mark on their own individual maps where the immigrants in the different stories and poems they read came from, and indicate when they came. In this way, Sandra is able to connect the literature to important social studies concepts.

Sandra's goals are to build new vocabulary and concepts through studying content areas such as geography. Keeping in mind that her students have not developed some concepts because they missed years of schooling, she spends time with her students studying basic geographic concepts.

> We also do a study on continents, oceans, and basic land forms such as mountains, riverbeds, deltas, canyons, and so forth. We do this by making an ABC book where students can draw pictures and write short definitions of the concepts.

The students also do a related art project, making a globe in the same way that piñatas are often made. They cover an inflated balloon with newspaper strips dipped in paste, let them dry, and paint the globe blue. Then they cut out the shapes of the continents and label them. Through cooperative discussion as they look at maps and the classroom globe, students help each other place the continents on the new globe and label the oceans. A piece of yellow yarn marks the equator. This globe-making project helps Sandra's students learn about geography. The globes are also used when studying other subject areas, including science and math, as the class learns about weather, the effects of water on land masses, and the percentage of water that makes up the earth.

Cinderella Around the World

A key to this multicultural immigrant theme is a comparative study of literature. Sandra and her students read and compare Cinderella stories from around the world. To introduce the Cinderella tales and to help her students build the necessary background concepts, such as the idea of royalty, Sandra begins with a limited text book, the humorous *Paperbag Princess*. The students do an art project connected to this book. Using yarn, cotton balls, glitter, and markers, they decorate a paper bag to create a princess of their own. Sandra's students enjoy this nontraditional story with its strong princess, who is so different from the female characters in traditional fairy tales and the traditional version of Cinderella.

Next, Sandra shows the students the many different Cinderella books from around the world that she has collected (Figure 4–4). She asks students to connect the idea of multicultural Cinderella books to the geography and social studies concepts they have been studying. Then she reads them a traditional and familiar version of Cinderella in Spanish.

Over the next days Sandra reads the students different Cinderella books from around the world. As a class, they talk about the differences among the books, including cultural differences and variations in plot, character, and setting. To follow up on these discussions, Sandra groups students heterogeneously according to their reading and English proficiency levels and gives each group a blank Venn diagram. Each group chooses two Cinderella books they wish to compare and fill in the diagram together.

The students also write their own Cinderella story together in the same way they wrote the class immigrant story: Students in groups decide on a title, a time period, setting, characters, main events, and an ending. Then the whole class writes a story together drawing on the group stories. One year the students wrote a Mexican Cinderella story because, at that time, there was not yet a published one. Their Mexican Cinderella tale had characteristics of students' Aztec and rural Mexican roots. Cinderella was named Ireri, in honor of the Aztec goddess of the rain, and wore glass *huaraches*

Ai-Ling, L. 1982. *Yen-Shen: A Cinderella Story from China.* New York: Philomel Books.

Busquets, C. 1986. *Cenicienta.* Mexico City: Ediciones Saro Mex.

Climo, S. 1989. *The Egyptian Cinderella.* New York: HarperCollins.

———. 1993. *The Korean Cinderella.* New York: HarperCollins.

———. 1999. *The Persian Cinderella.* New York: HarperCollins.

Coburn, J. 1996. *Jouanah: A Hmong Cinderella.* Fremont, CA: Shen's Books.

———. *Domitila: A Cinderella Tale from the Mexican Tradition.* Fremont, CA: Shen's Books.

Hickox, R. 1998. *The Golden Sandal.* New York: Holiday House.

Huck, C. 1989. *Princess Furball.* New York: Greenwillow Books.

Johnston, T. 1998. *Bigfoot Cinderrrrrella.* New York: G. P. Putnam's Sons.

Lum, D., and M. Nagano. 1994. *The Golden Slipper: A Vietnamese Legend.* New York: Troll Associates.

Martin, R. 1992. *The Rough-Face Girl.* New York: Putnam & Grosset.

Mehtal, L. 1985. *The Enchanted Anklet: A Cinderella Story from India.* Toronto, ON: Limur Publishing.

Munsch, R. *The Paperbag Princess.* Toronto, ON: Annick Press. Also published in Spanish as *La princesa vestida con una bolsa de papel* (1990).

Perlman, J. 1992. *Cinderella Penguin, or, the Little Glass Flipper.* New York: Scholastic.

Schroeder, A. 1994. *Lily and the Wooden Bowl.* New York: Bantam Doubleday Dell Publishing.

FIGURE 4–4.   *Cinderella Bibliography*

(sandals). When she did not get to go to the village festival, she went to the volcano to talk to the spirit, who directed her to an eagle's feather to get her wishes.

ABC Activity

Another activity Sandra uses in theme studies is an ABC activity. For example, in the immigrant theme study during a daily spelling/phonemic awareness time, students brainstorm the words connected to immigration they are learning. Sandra writes these words on a chart using the overhead projector. Usually, especially at the beginning of the year, Sandra has her students write down the words she writes and add their own words to make an alphabet book of vocabulary organized around the theme. Figure 4–5 shows the words Sandra and her students brainstormed for the immigrant theme.

ABC Chart — Topic: Immigration

A airplane America	B boat bus	C car clothes Cuba	D Documents	E Education Ellis Island	F Foot Freedom Food Flag
G government gate	H Hope House Hide History			I Immigrant illegal	J Jobs Justice
K Know-nothing	L liberty		TOPIC Immigration	M money	N night no oth Nation
O opportunity permission	P papers permission passport	Q Quilt	R Reunion (Family) Religion	S soldiers starts of slaves starving	T Trailer Train Trip
U United states	V Visa Vietnam violence valentía	W work walk War	X Mexico	Y New York	Z New Zealand

FIGURE 4–5. ABC Chart

Multicultural Corner and Recipe Book

Sandra uses two other activities in her immigrant theme study to help her students expand their understanding of the world, other cultures, and the value of their own culture. The first is the establishment of a classroom multicultural corner. The second is the creation of an international recipe book. For the multicultural corner, Sandra brings in Argentinian artifacts from her homeland, including a cup for drinking traditional *mate* tea, a travel brochure about the country, an Argentinian flag, and *dulce de leche*, a sweet used for making desserts. The students bring in items to represent their cultures, such as pottery, cooking utensils, costumes, and pictures of their families. They arrange all the objects on a table for their classmates and others in the school to look at and comment upon.

The recipe book serves as a celebration as well as a teaching tool. For each of the Cinderella stories, Sandra has the students copy down a recipe from that culture and then actually make and eat the food. So, for example, the class learns how to prepare teriyaki chicken with rice with an Asian Cinderella, tostadas with the Mexican Cinderella, pizza with the European Cinderella, and hummus with the Egyptian Cinderella. Sandra gives the students books with a world map on one page and a blank space for writing the recipe on the facing page. The students color in the country that goes with each recipe. They also bring in the ingredients and prepare the recipes. The excitement in the room as the students cook and eat dishes that, for the most part, are completely new to them is enough to show Sandra that her students have begun to feel comfortable in their classroom community and have started to gain the confidence they need for school.

Learning How to Learn

Sandra also follows the third key for success: She organizes collaborative activities and scaffolds instruction to build students' academic English proficiency. Her students learn how to learn during the initial immigrant theme study. She constantly works with them to help them develop English and develop concepts. She does this through literature, through scaffolding activities, through use of their first language, through skill building, through hands-on activities, and through meaningful group work. Every activity Sandra does with her students has a purpose.

Sandra realizes that she needs to help students build important academic concepts and literacy. For that reason, she uses many different kinds of graphic organizers to help scaffold their writing. During the immigrant theme study, for example, she provides a form for the home interviews, a language-experience activity, a form for groups to use to list story elements, various map activities, a time line, a comparison chart for the Cinderella stories, and the ABC chart for vocabulary building. All these graphic organizers help support students as they develop academic English.

Sandra's immigrant theme study illustrates all the reasons for organizing curriculum around themes based on big questions. Her students can make sense of the English language instruction because they know what the topic is. They learn about geography, math, social studies, and literature through the diverse but interconnected activities. They build vocabulary because words are constantly repeated during the theme study. The curriculum is engaging and teaches them important lessons about the lives and cultures of others, as well as helping them see how they fit into their new culture and the world. Sandra's immigrant theme study is an important beginning to helping her students develop cognitive, academic, and linguistic competence.

Spontaneous and Scientific Concepts

During the immigrant theme, Sandra helps her students develop the academic concepts and language they need to succeed in school. In Chapter 2 we explained that academic registers are characterized by specialized vocabulary and complex syntax. Academic language is context-reduced and cognitively demanding, in contrast to conversational language, which is context-embedded and cognitively undemanding.

Language and thinking are always intertwined. We can't easily think about things unless we have the language to express those thoughts. Vygotsky (1962) helped explain the relationship between thought and language. According to him, any word a child uses represents a generalization. For example, the child who says "dog" is using a word to label a type of animal. The word is a means of generalizing experience. At first, *dog* might represent a very general category that includes other animals, like cats and cows. Over time, children refine their understandings, and the words they use come to represent the same categories adults in their society use. The words represent concepts, and cognitive growth involves developing concepts that more closely match those of adults.

Words like *dog* are labels for what Vygotsky calls *spontaneous concepts*—concepts that arise naturally from everyday experience. Children develop these concepts in the course of growing up. They come to know the meaning of words like *dog* or *brother* if they have many experiences with animals and siblings. Spontaneous concepts are highly contextualized. The concepts are tied to the real-life experiences of the children. The language used to express spontaneous concepts is what Cummins (2000) calls *conversational language*. It is context-embedded and cognitively undemanding. All children develop spontaneous concepts and the language their cultural group uses to express those concepts.

Spontaneous concepts are contrasted with scientific concepts. *Dog* is a word that represents a spontaneous concept, while *mammal* represents a scientific concept. According to Kozulin:

> Spontaneous concepts emerge from the child's own reflections on immediate everyday experiences; they are rich but unsystematic and highly contextualized. Scientific concepts originate in the structures and specialized activity of classroom instruction and are characterized by systematic and logical organization. (in Cummins 2000, 60)

The process of education involves helping students develop the scientific concepts associated with each field of study. Scientific concepts organize everyday experience into a logical, interrelated order. Cummins notes that "the concepts themselves do not necessarily relate to scientific issues but their organization is 'scientific' in the sense of having a formal, logical and decontextualized structure" (60). For example, biologists categorize animals in different ways, such as *vertebrates* and *invertebrates* or *carnivores* and *herbivores*. These terms and the concepts they represent help organize our experience with animals in logical ways. These ways of thinking about animals are characteristic of academic language but are not commonly part of conversational language.

When Sandra teaches her students about geography, math, or literature, she helps them develop both academic concepts and the academic vocabulary people use to discuss those concepts. For example, in the study of literature she introduces terms like *plot, setting,* and *character*. The words represent academic concepts. Learning the vocabulary and learning the concept go hand in hand. She also introduces terms for shapes from geometry (*triangle, circle, square*) as students create quilts out of construction paper.

In addition to teaching her students some of the scientific concepts related to literature and geometry, during the immigrant unit Sandra introduces concepts from geography. Once students have developed spontaneous concepts to talk about rivers and mountains, Sandra can introduce the concept of water systems and landforms. Students know about the difference between villages, town, and cities. Sandra builds on this knowledge and extends it as she helps them develop concepts using terms such as *country, state,* and *county.* These terms represent legal or governmental divisions of land areas. They are scientific concepts in that they are related formally and logically within the legal system, but they would not develop naturally from commonsense observations, since some states are bigger than some countries, and while states are divided into counties, there is often no apparent reason that a certain area has been designated as a county. These scientific concepts are quite abstract, so Sandra uses hands-on activities and visual representations such as maps to try to make the concepts more comprehensible.

What English learners need is the academic language of school. Long-term English learners (LTELs) have often developed conversational language, and they can use it to discuss spontaneous concepts. However, both LTELs and recent immigrants with limited formal schooling generally lack scientific concepts and the academic language needed to comprehend and express those concepts. By teaching language through academic content organized around themes, teachers like Sandra help students develop the academic, cognitive, and linguistic proficiency they need to succeed in school.

During the theme studies, Sandra makes sure to embed the context-reduced academic language in a rich context by using visuals and hands-on activities. One danger of attempting to teach scientific concepts is to provide students with the labels for concepts they have not yet developed. Freire and Macedo (1987) write eloquently about this. They say that the words students read must connect to the world in which they live. Effective teachers always build scientific concepts on the spontaneous concepts the children bring to school. This is why it is so important to access students' background knowledge and experience. Sandra begins the year with her immigrant theme study because she knows she can use her students' experiences as immigrants as a springboard for introducing scientific concepts from literature, math, and geography.

Cummins' Interdependence Hypothesis

The academic language of schools is used to express scientific concepts. Students learn these concepts as they study different content areas—literature, math, science, and social studies. Some immigrant students, like those Sandra works with, have not developed these concepts because of their limited or interrupted formal schooling. They have a rich base of life experience, but a limited amount of school experience.

Long-term English learners (LTELs) have been in school but have not developed scientific concepts either. Many of these students come to school speaking a language other than English and receive much or all of their early instruction in English. Since the instruction is not comprehensible to them, they don't develop the academic language of school even though they may develop conversational English in their informal interactions in and out of school.

We have pointed out that recent immigrants with adequate formal schooling succeed at higher rates than either limited-formal-schooling students or LTELs. We can account for this difference in part by recognizing that immigrants with more schooling have already developed scientific concepts. Cummins (2000) has argued that these concepts transfer from one language to another because what students develop is a common underlying language proficiency. This claim that concepts transfer is known as the *interdependence hypothesis*. Cummins originally stated it in this way:

> To the extent that instruction in Lx is effective in promoting proficiency in Lx, transfer of this proficiency to Ly will occur provided there is adequate exposure to Ly (either in school or environment) and adequate motivation to learn Ly. (1981, 29)

What this means is that if students are effectively instructed in one language (*Lx*), the proficiency they develop in that language will transfer to a second language (*Ly*) as long as the students are exposed to the second language and are motivated to learn it. This interdependence hypothesis is based on the idea that a common cognitive/academic proficiency underlies any two languages. Transfer can occur once a student has developed enough proficiency in the second language to be able to comprehend and express the concepts already learned in the first language. Considerable research evidence on students in bilingual programs supports the idea of a common underlying proficiency. For example, G. García's (2000) review of the research showed that students who are literate in their first language do better in English.

The interdependence hypothesis helps explain why students who come to school with a strong academic background and literacy in their primary language achieve at high levels in English in a relatively short time. They already have the scientific concepts that they need. Their task is to learn the English words to express those concepts. Struggling older English learners, on the other hand, must learn both the concepts and the language.

Different cultural groups may organize experience differently. (For example, Canada is divided into provinces rather than states. The political leader is the prime minister, not the president, and elections are run quite differently than elections in the U.S.) However, the scientific concepts in many academic content areas are the same across cultures. This allows researchers from different countries to collaborate, and it allows students with previous schooling to do well in school.

Recently, Cummins has expanded his discussion of the interdependence hypothesis. He comments that the common underlying proficiency (CUP) may be thought of as a central processing system that consists of cognitive and linguistic abilities like memory, auditory discrimination, and abstract reasoning as well as specific conceptual and linguistic knowledge derived from experience and learning, such as vocabulary knowledge. Cummins states that the positive relationship between two languages comes from three sources:

1. the application of the same cognitive and linguistic abilities and skills to literacy development in both languages;
2. transfer of general concepts and knowledge of the world across languages in the sense that the individual's prior knowledge (in L1) represents the foundation of schemata upon which L2 acquisition is built; and
3. to the extent that the languages are related, transfer of specific linguistic features and skills across languages. (2000, 191)

Older English learners, including LFS students and LTELs, bring some scientific concepts that teachers can draw on. However, they may need more time and support to build the skills and knowledge, including scientific concepts, that are appropriate for students their age.

Accessing Cognates

Cummins points out that to the extent languages are related, specific features will transfer. Spanish and English are closely related languages, and teachers can draw on Spanish speakers' vocabulary in their first language to build the academic language they need in English. There are many cognates in Spanish and English. Cognates are words that are "born together"—that come from the same root. The words may be pronounced or spelled differently, but they are generally recognizable across languages. For example, the English word *alphabet* is *alfabeto* in Spanish.

Although English is a Germanic language, many of the scholarly terms in the English vocabulary have Latin and Greek roots. According to Corson (1995), about 60 percent of the words used in English texts come from Greek and Latin sources. In Chapter 2 we pointed out that most words in conversational English come from Anglo-Saxon roots, but academic English is made up largely of Latin and Greek borrowings. Since Spanish derives from Latin, many common words in Spanish are scientific words in English. Teachers can help Spanish speakers develop academic language by making connections between everyday Spanish terms and English academic vocabulary.

Williams (2001) suggests that teachers "draw attention visually to Spanish cognates . . . by using an overhead projector. Do not assume that students will make the connections about these cognates automatically" (751). She also states that teachers can create a classroom cognate wall or dictionary. Students can add to the list of words on the wall or in the dictionary throughout the year. Williams also provides examples of cognates taken from NTC's dictionary of Spanish cognates. Figure 4–6 shows some of the English-Spanish cognates that are used in the study of history.

Rodríguez (2001) also advocates using cognates to teach Spanish speakers. He suggests specific strategy lessons designed to increase students' awareness of cognates. For example, after reading a short passage and discussing the content, students can work in pairs to identify English-Spanish cognates in the passage. Students can be given a second version of the text in which

English	Spanish
civilization	civilizacíon
history	historia
past	pasado
pioneer	pionero
colonial	colonial
diary	diario

FIGURE 4–6. *English-Spanish Cognates*

the cognates are replaced by words with Germanic roots. Students can figure out the new words by comparing them with the cognates. What is important in lessons like this is to focus students' attention specifically on language features, such as cognates, that they can later use to increase their understanding of academic texts in English.

Rodríguez provides a helpful list of the types of English-Spanish cognates that teachers might present. He notes that some words have the same spelling in both languages (*hotel*); some are spelled nearly the same with predictable variations (*contaminacíon*); some are less apparently related but share the same root (*sport, deporte*); some sound alike even though the spellings vary (*pleasure, placer*); and some are cognates for one meaning but not for another (*letter, letra* [of the alphabet]; *letter, carta* [written correspondence]). It is good for students to be alert to these different types of cognates. Teachers may also ask students to find regular differences between the two languages. For example, the English suffix *-tion* usually appears in Spanish as *-cíon*.

The articles by Rodríguez and Williams include helpful ideas for teaching students about cognates. One point that Cummins makes is that transfer of knowledge and skills, such as the knowledge of cognates, does not occur automatically. Teachers need to facilitate the process with specific lessons. Williams suggests that teachers plan lessons that have language objectives as well as content objectives. Since language and content are closely related, this is sound advice. Teachers can help students develop scientific concepts and academic language by teaching language through content and by being aware that they are always both language teachers and academic-content teachers.

Other Relevant Themes

Sandra developed a theme with her students that connected to their lives and helped them academically. Other teachers working with older students have developed themes around different relevant questions. Oscar, the high school teacher we introduced in Chapter 1, teaches a yearlong theme around the question "How do we deal with oppression?" He finds that almost all the reading and discussions that he and his students do together relate to this big question. In Chapter 5, we give examples of the activities Oscar does with his classes during this theme study.

We have written in other books about Mary's sense-of-self and migrant theme studies, Lonna's AIDS theme study, and Silvio and Sandra's agriculture theme study (Freeman and Freeman 1996, 1998a, 2001). Each of these theme studies met the needs of older students, many of whom were long-term English learners or had had limited formal schooling.

Mary's Sense-of-Self Theme

Mary developed her sense-of-self theme for her ninth graders. The integrated curriculum helped her students answer the big question "Who am I?" Mary chose this theme because she knew that for her students to appreciate the diversity in their school and their world, they should first understand themselves. Some of her students were newcomer Punjabis and Hispanics with various levels of previous schooling. Others were Hispanics who had been in the school system since kindergarten. All her students became involved in this theme. They got to know themselves and each other through interviews, making personal coats of arms, writing poetry about themselves and their goals, and graphing the high and low points in their personal histories. Throughout the theme study they read pieces of literature and responded by writing in different genres. For example, after reading "My Name," a chapter from *The House on Mango Street* (Cisneros 1984), students researched the meaning of their own names, made posters, and presented what they had learned to the class.

Mary's sense-of-self theme study and the migrant experience theme study she developed helped her students gain the reading and writing skills they needed. Mary explained something that's a problem for struggling English learners:

> The biggest reason that these students have so much trouble in school is that people think they are proficient in reading and writing English just because they speak English. Once this assumption is made, the trouble begins. (Freeman and Freeman 1998a, 45)

In her migrant theme, Mary had her students, many of whom were children of migrant workers, explore the question "What is the migrant experience and how does it influence our lives?" They studied this theme through reading literature, including poetry, short essays, and picture books. Some of the books Mary used were *A Migrant Family* (Brimmer 1992), *Earth Angels* (Buirski 1994), *Here Is My Kingdom: Hispanic-American Literature and Art for Young People* (Duran 1994), and Cisneros' *The House on Mango Street*. Once they had built enough background knowledge about the migrant experience, the class read, discussed, and wrote about the required novel, *The Grapes of Wrath* (Steinbeck 1967).

Lonna's AIDS Theme

Lonna, an ESL teacher in an urban high school, worked with her class of mostly Southeast Asian students on the topic of AIDS. After a discussion about a local Hmong man who had committed suicide because he believed he had the disease, it was clear that the students had many misconceptions about AIDS. Answering the question "What is AIDS and how do we fight it?" became important and relevant for Lonna's students.

The class explored this topic together through a number of activities. They read newspaper and magazine articles as well as more technical reports about AIDS. Lonna brought in a guest speaker who presented information and answered students' questions. She also found an educational video to show to and discuss with her students. Students wrote journal entries that Lonna responded to, and also wrote a longer paper to summarize their understanding of this important topic. Through this focused reading and writing, the students developed some of the scientific concepts and academic language they needed for school success.

Silvio and Sandra's Theme—The Importance of Agriculture

Silvio and Sandra both brought the theme of agriculture and its importance to their migrant students. With his third and fourth graders, almost all of whom have experienced and continue to experience interrupted schooling, Silvio introduces the question "Why is agriculture important?" and develops concepts and language through bilingual poetry and short essays. Poetry and essays are ideal for his students who are acquiring literacy because the texts are short and accessible.

Ada has written a number of books filled with wonderful poems about the lives of Latinos. For example, *Gathering the Sun* (1997) is a richly illustrated bilingual alphabet book. Each page has a poem in Spanish and in English on a topic that relates to the lives of migrant workers, such as picking peaches. Similarly, Garza's books (1990, 1996) focus on the life experiences of Latinos. She tells familiar stories drawn from her life growing up in Texas and playing with horned toads or cleaning *nopales*, topics the students relate to. Each short essay is accompanied by a colorful illustration that provides contextual support for the reading.

In the same way, Sandra helps her students see the importance of agriculture through her extended From the Field to the Table unit (Freeman and Freeman 2001). Her students answer questions including "How do plants grow?"; "How do products get to the store?"; and "What is good nutrition?" They study plant growth, how products are brought to the market, and the nutritional value of different foods. They read *Where Does Breakfast Come From?* (Flint 1998) and discuss where breakfast items such as eggs, cereal, milk, and juice come from. Sandra concludes the theme study by reading literature books about foods students enjoy, like strawberry shortcake (Stevens and Crummel 1999), apple pie (Thompson 1997), tamales (Soto 1993), sandwiches (Stoodt 1997), and cookies (Tatler 1993), along with unusual foods, like thundercake (Polacco 1990). She has the students choose one of the books, find all the ingredients for the featured dish, and trace how the ingredients get from the field to the table. The students include recipes for the dishes they have chosen. Naturally, during the final celebration, students follow the recipes and make the food for the whole class to share. Like the other teachers mentioned, Sandra uses literature, hands-on activities, extensive reading and writing, and a variety of strategies to help her limited-formal-schooling newcomers construct meaning in English and develop academic competence.

Linda's Coming to America Theme
One other theme study was carried out by Linda, an experienced secondary ESL and Spanish teacher with an M.A. in bilingual education. Linda

is constantly trying to meet her students' needs and push their thinking. During one summer session, she taught a class of Southeast Asian and Hispanic long-term English learners who had conversational fluency in English but lacked the academic literacy they needed to compete with native speakers. The theme question for that class was "How has coming to and living in the U.S. changed you and your family?" To build community at the beginning of the summer session, Linda had students bring their favorite fruits to class to make a salad. She explains what happened:

> The task was to have each student bring just one piece of fruit for our salad, but I found that like eating chips, no one could bring just *one*, and so small bags of apples, oranges, lemons appeared on THE DAY along with clusters of grapes, two or three bananas, and other things in season. The teacher supplied the paper goods, spoons, cutting board and knives. Everybody worked. Some chopped, some mixed, some served and *everybody* cleaned up.
>
> Building community allowed students to more freely share through reading, writing, and talking about differences in diet, clothes, and traditions. They began to really think about why people come to this country and what happens once they get here.

The class read a short chapter book, *My Name Is María Isabel* (Ada 1993), which deals with being an immigrant in U.S. schools, and Linda read aloud chapters from *Hello, My Name Is Scrambled Eggs* (Gilson 1966) and parts of *Voices from the Fields* (Atkin 1993), both books that help students think about and talk about their roots and what it is like adjusting to U.S. culture. She also read relevant pictures books, like *Going Home* (Bunting 1996), a powerful story about a family's return to Mexico for Christmas told from the perspective of a young boy who has lost his connection to his roots. Linda and her students discussed how the boy came to understand that his parents had sacrificed their own lives and given up their native country to give their children opportunities. Linda used various scaffolding devices, including Venn diagrams and other graphic organizers, to help students develop concepts and build their academic language. Daily activities during this theme study included journaling and writers workshop. These writing activities led to the culminating project for the six-week session, the production of a bound collection of student-authored stories and poems, called *Summer Stories*. The class ended as it began, with the sharing of food. This time it was a community meal where finished stories and poems were shared and students passed around their copies of the collection to be signed by the authors.

Thematic Instruction in Secondary Schools

In Chapter 3, we reviewed the research on effective practices for English learners. Thematic instruction is consistent with all the research recommendations. The first key for success is to engage students in challenging, theme-based activities (Figure 1–2). Peregoy and Boyle (2001) explain the importance of themes for English learners in this way:

> The meaningful context established by the theme supports the comprehensibility of instruction, thereby increasing both content learning and second language acquisition. In addition, theme-based collaborative projects create student interest, motivation, involvement, and purpose. (79)

Many teachers in middle and secondary schools have been reluctant to implement theme studies because they teach single subjects and do not see how organizing around themes is useful or even possible. However, some teachers of older students have worked together to organize curriculum thematically across academic disciplines. These efforts have made a difference for students, including English language learners. In the following sections, we describe some of these whole-school programs.

The Explorer Team

One group of inner-city seventh- and eighth-grade teachers formed the Explorer Team to engage their diverse students in activities that had meaning and purpose for them (Freeman and Freeman 2001). The teachers integrated language arts, history, math, and science for a group of 140 students around the question "How are we part of one world, one family?" Kathy, one of the teachers, explained the goal for the students:

> We strive for them to see themselves as part of one human family with cultural, language, and ethnic diversity as positive and beneficial to the well-being and fulfillment of all people. (122)

One project that integrated the academic areas and helped students see each other as part of a family involved the eighth graders in making "survival kits" for incoming seventh graders. These kits included notes with general advice, maps of the school, and graphed survey results about relevant topics such as favorite brands of clothing, favorite foods to eat on campus, and favorite noontime activities.

Another activity that all the teachers and students participated in was a career day. Students prepared by reading in language arts about a variety of careers; studying the economic aspects of careers in math class, including reading graphs and charts; and reviewing science career options during science class. The history teacher taught students to conduct computer searches on careers and their origins. On the day the speakers arrived, students were prepared to listen and ask questions. They were inspired by the speakers, who represented the rich diversity of the community and the school, including an African American principal, an Hispanic sociology professor, and a Hmong woman who had just given the commencement address for her university.

At the eighth-grade graduation, the students from the Explorer Team received 90 percent of all the awards given, including academic, athletic, and citizenship awards. Though the teachers and the students had worked hard, the results were worth it. As Kathy reported,

> At the end of the ceremony everyone—teachers, administrators, parents, and the students themselves—marveled together. Something very special had happened with the group. They had bonded as they learned. The students had begun as a diverse group of inner-city average to below-average students from many different backgrounds. Few thought much about their futures, and if they did, they did not consider college. When they graduated, they were students with expectations, students with determination, students with hope, and especially students with a future. (Freeman and Freeman 2001, 125)

Project Theme

Research projects at secondary schools in which university researchers collaborate with teachers have produced some exciting results. E. García (1999) tells about a time he was giving a presentation about his effective schools research and mentioned thematic instruction and other strategies for English language learners. A middle-school principal challenged García to come to his school and improve the curriculum for the English learners there. García took the challenge and led a project at that middle school, called Project Theme. Teachers of reading, English, science, mathematics, and social studies worked together to create a thematic, integrated curriculum. The teachers participated in preservice and inservice training, met monthly with researchers and each other, and observed in one another's classrooms.

The students were divided into two cohorts. English learners were included in each group. The strategies that the effective schooling research called for and that the teachers used included thematic, integrated curriculum; emphasis on small-group activities incorporating heterogeneous grouping and peer tutoring; emphasis on literacy activities such as interactive journals and interactive literature study; use of cooperative learning strategies; and emphasis on strategies that fostered equal-status interactions. Through what they learned during the inservices and their own discussions, the teachers, working with the researchers, realized that both a strong curriculum and the inclusion of activities that fostered students' self-esteem were essential. As a result, they developed strategies to help build the students' self-image, including recognition of achievement in individual and group work; study of conflict and the development of problem-solving skills; and lessons that promoted understanding and appreciation of individual and cultural differences.

Teachers and students working together developed several themes: the Olympics, the fine arts, the ocean, crime and nonviolence, careers, gender, AIDS, and ethnic identity. These themes encouraged both language and literacy development. As they studied these cross-disciplinary themes, students also developed academic knowledge and skills.

To evaluate Project Theme, standardized tests in English and language-assessment tests were administered to both the Project Theme students and control groups. In addition, interview data about the students' academic self-concepts and social identities were gathered. García reported the overall results of the project. Project Theme students had more positive views of ethnic identity, both their own and that of others, than other students had, and positive self-esteem. They also had consistently positive visions for their future, including plans for future schooling, and positive academic results. As García wrote,

> The results of the project are clearly positive. That is, the data show consistently more positive outcomes for the theme students compared to those in the school's conventional program. Most notably, comparative analyses in reading comprehension, vocabulary, language mechanics, and language expression in English significantly favored the theme students. (1999, 354)

Project Theme, then, had similar results to the Explorer Team project described in the previous section: Students had improved academic achievement and more positive views of themselves and of diversity.

Project Avance

Project Avance (Spanish for *advance*) was a high school research project modeled after Project Theme (E. García 1999). The strategies employed were exactly the same as those for Project Theme. In addition, the teachers and the school's principal visited the Project Theme site. In this program, sixty English language learners were identified as being highly motivated. Teachers in the program insisted that these students receive the same curriculum as mainstream students. They did not want to water down the curriculum.

The curriculum was not transformed as it had been for Project Theme, but the teachers did institute student-generated themes and used many strategies, which they agreed made a difference in working with their English learners, to make the academic input comprehensible. The strategies included using visuals, to connect content to real-world experiences, using music and drama, having students write in journals and learning logs, and connecting content through thematic units.

One of the key findings that the researchers reported was a change in teacher attitude. Teachers began to look at student achievement differently, to assess student work by looking at projects rather than test scores, to value the opportunity to share teaching ideas with each other, to approach the teaching of content in alternate ways, to confront issues such as race relations, and to realize that all students, including English learners, need challenging academic content.

International High School

Perhaps the best known of all the high schools that have implemented an innovative theme-based curriculum is International High School in New York City (Freeman and Freeman 1998a). Located in LaGuardia Community College in Queens, this high school is made up entirely of immigrant students who, in order to qualify for admission, must have lived in the United States less than four years and scored below the 20th percentile on an English language proficiency exam. Ninety-five percent of the students graduate and 90 percent are accepted to postsecondary schools. At the end of the first three years of the International High School program, the dropout rate was only 3.9 percent and all 54 members of the first senior class were accepted to college (Darling-Hammond, Ancess, and Falk 1995).

The school's faculty and students believe that the key to the success of this program is the collaborative learning and sharing that take place:

> International is committed to viewing teachers and students . . . as resources for each other, using participation in decision making and collective action as the basis for growth and development. (115)

A central feature of this program is the emphasis on career education. Two of the eight statements of the school's philosophy reflect this goal:

- the carefully planned use of multiple learning contexts in addition to the classroom (e.g. learning centers, career internship sites, field trips), facilitates language acquisition and content area mastery.
- career education is a significant motivational factor for adolescent learners. (Lucas 1997, 197)

The program is designed to help students connect school studies with life in America beyond the school setting. Students learn the interpersonal skills needed to function in the workplace during internships. They prepare for the internships through their course work. For example, for one internship they study a thematic unit called The American Dream, followed by an internship course called The American Reality.

The career internship is built into two of the school's twelve interdisciplinary theme clusters. Students' preparation for internships includes reflecting on their values, interests, and abilities; getting information about different careers and available internships; developing a résumé; learning about and practicing interviews; learning about expectations, norms, and ways of relating in workplaces in the United States; and reflecting on obstacles to their careers of interest as well as available support systems. Students respond positively to this experience, even though it is difficult:

> "It's scary at first, but it helps you learn English and build your confidence."
>
> "It gives you work experience. You learn more about the subject."
>
> "It helps you know about real life when you finish college." (Lucas 1997, 200)

English as a second language is not taught as a separate course. Groups of approximately seventy-five students work together in a cluster with four to eight staff members over a period of three semesters. All students learn English by studying meaningful content and by working together in small multilingual, multicultural groups. "Their tasks are structured so that they must communicate ideas and directions to one another as they collaboratively produce and evaluate their work" (Darling-Hammond, Ancess, and Falk 1995, 118). Students can use the first language socially and in class, and many who lack literacy choose to develop their first languages by taking further course work (Lucas 1996).

Classes are organized around twelve interdisciplinary themes on topics such as diversity, interdependence, democracy, and government participation. Traditional subject-area content is included in each theme. For example, the "motion" theme combines a literature course with an integrated math and physics course and a physical education course called Project Adventure, which is modeled after Outward Bound. The three courses are unified through the focus on motion.

Students from fifty-four countries speaking thirty-nine different languages have come together at International High School and worked with faculty and other students to demonstrate how sharing in their learning improves academics. This program, with its interactive, theme-based focus, gives us hope that a diverse society can collaborate, as these students and faculty have, achieve academically, and learn to succeed in our society.

Conclusion

The teachers highlighted in this chapter and the programs described all have certain things in common, including organization around a relevant and meaningful theme with a universal appeal, attempts to integrate content from different subject areas, and development of scientific concepts and academic language. When working with struggling older English learners, it is important to organize curriculum around themes based on big questions. The first key for success is to engage students in challenging, theme-based activities. By doing that, the teachers we have described in this chapter have helped their older English learners succeed and begin to close the achievement gap.

Professional Extensions

1. Two of the themes that Sandra uses with her newcomer rural students are centered on the questions "How do I fit in as an immigrant?" and "How do products get from the field to the table?" Select a group of English language learners in your school or classroom and suggest four or five big questions for them. In a short paragraph, explain why those questions would be relevant to them.

2. Chose one relevant theme for a group of English learners. Build a list of appropriate literature and content books that you might use in teaching that theme.

3. Chose one relevant theme for a group of English learners. Choose two or three graphic organizers you might use with the students in developing the theme. Explain what scientific concepts the graphic organizers help to support.

4. Sandra developed scientific concepts for her students related to land forms, literary terms, and patterns. Choose a specific content area and list several scientific concepts that you might develop with your students.

5. The interdependence hypothesis says that we can access what we already know when we are learning something new. If you have studied a second language, relate how your knowledge of English (or other first language) helped you in learning the second language. What knowledge or information did you transfer?

6. We discussed how cognates in Spanish can help native Spanish speakers access academic language. If you are working with native Spanish speakers, choose an academic reading from your subject area. Work with your students to show them what cognates are and show them a few cognates within the reading. Then have the students work in pairs or small groups to find others. Have them report back. Write up how this experience went.

7. We described two junior high school programs where teachers from different subject areas worked together on themes. Do you know of other junior high or high schools doing this? Find out about the program and describe it.

8. The International High School in New York has a very exciting curriculum for newcomer students. What do you see as benefits of a program like this for your newcomer students? What would be the barriers to establishing such a program?

Using Routines and Strategies to Scaffold Instruction

What do you want your teacher to know about you as a reader and writer?

♦ *That I need a lot of help to improve in everything.*

♦ *To read I know but not as much as the other kids. I don't know how to writ long and hard words. To learn I have to listen when the teacher is talking and listen when he is givin lesson.*

♦ *I would like my teacher to know that I don't know lot of reading because I don't speaked all that inglish.*

How do you feel about what you write?

♦ *I feel kind of engry because I don't know how to write correctly.*

♦ *That I don't know how to write.*

What are your memories of learning to read in your first or second language?

♦ *I never leard how to read because I never pay attention to the teacher and never read at school or at my house.*

♦ *My memories of learning to read is whe I was in thrird grade my teacher was very helpfull and I started by learning the alphabet.*

♦ *Well, I can't remember my memories well I only could say that I had a lot of trouble on learning english, but now look at me NOW I can do anything now.*

Can you skim a textbook chapter in 5–10 minutes and figure out the major points covered?

♦ *No, when I read the textbook I don't remember about I read.*

♦ *I heat reading and I don't under stand.*

These questions and answers come from a survey that Oscar gives the students in his ninth-grade reading and language arts classes at the beginning of each semester. The final response sadly summarizes what many of Oscar's students feel as they begin this class. They struggle with writing, they hate to read, and they don't understand what they read.

Many of Oscar's students are what we have described earlier as long-term English learners (LTELs). A few are native English speakers and a few are newcomers. All of the students are in his classes because they have struggled academically. Oscar's goal is to engage his students in meaningful reading and writing and help them develop strategies to comprehend both literature and content-area texts.

Oscar's teaching reflects both the third and fourth keys to success (Figure 1–2). He organizes collaborative activities and scaffolds instruction, and he builds students' confidence. Oscar accomplishes this by incorporating a variety of strategies and activities into his daily classroom routine. He works hard to give students the strategies they need, and he also works to build their confidence so they can value themselves as readers and writers. Oscar's goal is that at the end of the year all his students will respond with "I can do anything now!"

Components of Effective Teaching

Gersten and Jiménez (1994) have reviewed research in a wide variety of fields—cognitive strategies, approaches to literature instruction, programs in bilingual education and second-language acquisition, and effective instruction for at-risk students—to develop specific suggestions for English learners. They identify eight constructs of effective instruction that are important for teachers to keep in mind as they plan their lessons (Figure 5–1).

The first two constructs, *challenge* and *involvement*, are components of the first key for success. Teachers must engage students in activities that involve them and make them think. *Success*, the third construct, is similar to the fourth key. With success, students begin to build their self-confidence. Success in schools also helps students value schooling. Constructs three through seven reflect components of the third key, organizing collaborative groups and scaffolding instruction. Effective teachers consistently use a variety of techniques to give students access to content knowledge. Students can provide scaffolds for one another and thus mediate instruction when teachers plan collaboration among students. During cooperative activities such as jigsaw or think/pair/share (Kagan 1986, 1988), students can help each other construct meaning from expository texts and understand difficult concepts. Teachers who are knowledgeable in bilingual education and second-language acquisition are familiar with using strategies to make lan-

Constructs for Effective Instruction
1. Challenge
2. Involvement
3. Success
4. Scaffolding/cognitive strategies
5. Mediation/feedback
6. Collaborative/cooperative learning
7. Techniques for second-language acquisition/sheltered English
8. Respect for cultural diversity

FIGURE 5–1. *Constructs for Effective Instruction (adapted from Gersten and Jiménez 1994)*

guage and content comprehensible (see Figure 3–1). The eighth construct, like the second key, emphasizes the importance of recognizing and building on students' backgrounds. When teachers draw on these strengths, they help older English learners begin to close the achievement gap.

Drawing on the work of Gersten and Jiménez, the effective instruction research by E. García (1991, 1999) discussed in Chapter 3, and a longitudinal study on bilingual education by Ramírez (1991), Saunders, O'Brien, Lennon, and McLean (1999) identify four theoretical premises to promote first- and second-language acquisition and academic achievement:

1. Challenge: Consistently challenge students academically. Challenge them to think, learn, and engage intellectually.
2. Comprehensiveness: Address both meaning and skills, promote both higher level thinking and appropriate drill and practice, and provide complementary portions of student- and teacher-centeredness.
3. Continuity: Achieve continuity in curriculum and instruction as students move from primary to middle to upper grades and from Spanish to English language arts.
4. Connections: Build upon and make explicit the connections between students' existing knowledge, skills, and experiences and the academic curriculum to be learned (including language, literacy, and content). (2)

These four premises, which are consistent with the keys for success, underlie any sound instructional plan for older English learners. Students must be challenged to engage in academic studies. The fact that students are limited in their English proficiency does not mean that they are limited in their thinking ability, and they must be pushed to engage with difficult ideas. The curriculum must be comprehensive and deal with both academic concepts and the specific skills needed to access those concepts. Valdés (2001) found that the curriculum given to the English learners she studied was neither challenging nor comprehensive, and students were not prepared to handle the academics of mainstream classes. In her recommendations Valdés stresses the importance of giving students access to the curriculum while they are learning English—that is, giving them the academic English they need to study grade level–appropriate coursework.

The curriculum must also have continuity. One problem that many long-term English learners have experienced is a lack of continuity. They have been in and out of bilingual, ESL, and mainstream classes. As students move from upper-elementary to middle school and again from middle to high school, systems need to be in place so that teachers receive information about the incoming students. Curriculum should be articulated across languages and grade levels. Finally, as we have shown in the previous chapters, good teaching involves making connections between students' background experiences and the academic content they are expected to learn.

The suggestions that Saunders, O'Brien, Lennon, and McLean offer and the constructs listed by Gersten and Jiménez are reflected in the four keys we have developed (Figure 1–2). There is considerable consensus among researchers about how best to help older English learners close the achievement gap and succeed academically. When teachers implement practices that are consistent with the research recommendations, they provide all their students with greater opportunities to succeed. One feature of effective classrooms is a consistent routine.

Routines

English learners benefit when teachers establish daily routines. Recent arrivals with limited or interrupted schooling may not have learned how schools work or how students are expected to respond to typical class activities. Limited-formal-schooling (LFS) students are constantly trying to understand what is expected of them. Often schools in this country are so different from their previous experiences that they go through culture shock and cannot participate even when they do understand the instruction.

When there is a classroom routine, English learners feel more relaxed because they know the kinds of activities they should be engaged in and what it is they are supposed to do during certain times of the day or the period. As they become familiar with the structure of the school day and the daily activities, they spend less mental energy figuring out what they are supposed to be doing. This leaves more mental space for them to comprehend the language and content of the class.

Routines are also helpful to long-term English learners (LTELs). These students have been in schools in this country for a long time without experiencing academic success. Many of them have given up trying because they think they cannot succeed. Teachers we have worked with have found that if there are predictable routines, activities the students can count on each day, they are more comfortable in taking risks to meet the language and academic content challenges they face.

In this chapter we describe in detail the daily routines of two successful teachers, Oscar, who works primarily with LTELs, and Sandra, most of whose students are LFS. We also explain several of the strategies they use to help scaffold their students' learning, and we describe the kinds of materials they provide. Effective teachers establish predictable routines, employ a variety of strategies, and find appropriate materials for their older English learners.

Oscar's Daily Routine

"R.I.O.T." and "Torture" are part of the day for students in Oscar's reading and language arts classes. Having a daily routine helps provide the continuity they need. In addition, Oscar organizes instruction thematically around big questions. For example, this year he and his students have explored the question "How do we deal with oppression?" Having a thematic focus adds more consistency to daily classes.

Oscar's high school uses a block schedule. As a result, Oscar sees each of his classes for one hour and thirty-five minutes daily. Oscar makes good use of these longer blocks of time. His students, as the responses at the opening of the chapter show, are reluctant readers and writers when they begin his class, but through following the daily routine, they soon become involved and enthusiastic about learning. Figure 5–2 shows Oscar's daily schedule. In the following sections, we explain the components of his routine.

Opening and R.I.O.T.

Oscar begins each class with a five-minute "talk time." Students are allowed to talk together about anything they want. He says, "I let them get whatever social, personal things that are on their minds out of the way so we can concentrate on the content of the class." Then Oscar takes attendance and announcements are read over the school loudspeaker.

During sustained silent reading (SSR) time, which Oscar and his students call R.I.O.T. (Reading Is Our Thing), the students read books of their choice for twenty minutes. Many of Oscar's students are in his reading class because they dislike reading and have not done much of it. Oscar explains:

> Many of my students struggled early on in their schooling with reading that was taught through phonics and worksheets. The solution was

Oscar's Daily Class Schedule	
Opening	• Talk time • Greeting • Attendance • Announcements
R.I.O.T. (Reading Is Our Thing)	• Students read • Teacher involves students in literature studies and gives assessments and small-group instruction
Homework Review	• Review homework • Answer questions • Reflect and evaluate • Turn in homework
Choral Reading	• Monday: Pick a group and a poem • Tuesday and Thursday: Practice for seven minutes • Friday: Perform!
Torture	• Teacher and students talk about reading theory and work together on effective reading and writing strategies
Literature	• Core work: All students have a copy of the text. The teacher reads and students respond in a variety of ways.
Writers Workshop	• Minilesson: Drawing on student needs, teacher responds • Workshop: Prewriting, rough draft, peer conferencing, final draft, publishing, idea incubation, and starting the cycle all over!
Closing	• Explain the homework • Students write assignments and upcoming events on calendars • Various language-play activities to build vocabulary

FIGURE 5–2. *Oscar's Daily Class Schedule*

to give them more phonics and worksheets. They seldom had the opportunity to get involved in reading.

Oscar has built a large classroom library filled with a variety of high-interest adolescent literature to ensure that his students have books to read. In addition, the library includes picture books, newspapers in both Spanish and English, and magazines such as *U.S. News and World Report, Newsweek, Sports Illustrated, Teen People, Teen, Skateboard, The Source, Vibe, YM (Your Magazine), Slam,* and *Mh18 (Men's Health 18).*

Oscar knows that access to interesting reading materials is what gets people reading. McQuillan (1998) reports on several studies that show that access to books leads to increased reading. In one study (Ramos and Krashen 1998), the researchers found that taking elementary school children who had little exposure to books to the library made a huge difference in their reading and interest in reading. Oscar's students attended rural elementary schools where there was limited library access and the emphasis was not on reading but on skills. For most of the students, reading for pleasure was not part of the school day before they reached Oscar's class.

In fact, the two junior highs that most of Oscar's students attend have recently adopted a reading program that uses a readability formula to evaluate books. Students are allowed to read only the books that are at their level. They are tested on each book that they read. This is a very controlled program that is based on questionable research. Many students come to see reading as getting through a book to answer questions. Oscar, in contrast, is trying to help students value reading for its intrinsic value rather than to complete reading solely for extrinsic rewards. His students' experience in the junior high program only makes his job more difficult.

Worthy (1996) found that middle-school students who read infrequently reported that they had limited access to books of interest at home and a lack of reading choice and opportunities to read for pleasure at school. These students did not dislike reading, but they did lack reading materials. McQuillan (1998) cities studies that show that the numbers of books available to students depends on their socioeconomic status. Most of Oscar's students come from low-income families and have few age-appropriate books in their homes.

Feitelson and Goldstein (1986) reported large differences in the numbers of age-appropriate books in the homes of middle-income and low-income children. There were ten times as many books in the middle-class homes. Raz and Bryant (1990) found that differences in the numbers of books owned and the number of visits to the library by children who were not yet reading independently was related to economic status. Middle-income children had three times as many books at home, and made about three times as many visits to the library each month, as low-income children.

Smith, Constantino, and Krashen (1996) studied differences in access to books in the home, school, and community in three areas of Los Angeles. This study revealed huge differences in print access between economically depressed communities and high-income areas. For example, children in Beverly Hills homes had an average of 199 age-appropriate books in their homes compared to 2.7 books per child in Compton and 0.4 books per child in Watts. The students with the fewest books in their homes also had the fewest books in classroom, school, and public libraries. Beverly Hills classrooms had an average of 392 books compared to Compton's 47 and Watts' 54. School libraries in Beverly Hills had an average of 60,000 volumes, while those in Watts had 23,000 and Compton school libraries had only 16,000. Beverly Hills' public library had 200,600 volumes, about double the number of the 110,00 in Watts or the 90,000 in Compton. Not surprisingly, the communities where students had the fewest books in their homes also had fewer bookstores.

This phenomenon is not limited to California. A study by Allington, Guice, Baker, Michaelson, and Li (1995) showed that there were fewer books per child in the libraries of schools that served more poor children. In addition, schools that served many poor children allowed fewer visits to the school libraries.

Oscar's students have a rich selection of books to choose from. During R.I.O.T. time they read from a collection of over five hundred books, as well as newspapers and magazines. As they read, Oscar works with individuals and small groups teaching minilessons, doing assessments, and leading literature studies.

Homework Review and Choral Reading

Homework review time is an important part of Oscar's daily routine. While the assignments vary, many require written responses to expository texts, usually articles from newspapers and news magazines such as *U.S. News and World Report, Time,* and *Newsweek.* These articles center on current events of interest that connect to Oscar's yearlong theme questions. Sometimes the students find the articles they respond to, but often Oscar has articles to give them. In fact, Oscar is constantly supported by colleagues who know what his theme for the year is and leave relevant articles in his box or send him articles with notes saying things like, "We thought you and your students would be interested in this one."

For homework, Oscar's students read the articles and respond by looking for key ideas, showing places in the articles where the key ideas are supported, and identifying the author's intent by deciding, for example, if the article is meant to inform or persuade. There is time in this part of the daily routine for students to share what they read and responded to and to evaluate how they responded. After discussion and sometimes revision of their work, they turn in their assignments.

For a change of pace, students then move to a different kind of activity, choral reading. The different stages of this activity culminate in a presentation each Friday. Choral reading has several benefits for English learners, especially for older learners who may be self-conscious about their pronunciation of English. Students rehearse and present the readings together, so no one student is put on the spot. Poetry is a good resource for choral reading because the content can be significant but the reading is short and less intimidating than an article or a book. Reading poetry helps students develop the intonation rhythms of English.

On Monday the students form groups and choose a poem or a poem-like reading, such as a rap, that they wish to perform. Oscar's students have used poems from *Cool Salsa: Bilingual Poems on Growing Up Latino in the United States* (Carlson 1994), poetry and essays from *My Own True Name* (Mora 2000), and rap from CDs. The late rapper Tupac Shakur is one favorite of the students. *The Rose That Grew from Concrete* (1999), a book of his poetry with a foreword by Nikki Giovanni and an introduction by Leila Steinberg, Tupac's manager, has been an especially popular choice for performances.

On Tuesdays and Thursdays, Oscar gives the students exactly seven minutes, which he carefully times, to practice for their Friday presentation. On Fridays they perform. Oscar noted:

> Students developed a four-point choral presentation rubric. As they watch the presentations they evaluate themselves as well as their classmates. Another interesting feature of this activity is how the presentations evolve throughout the year. They get quite sophisticated with props, intonations, and multimedia.

The props did in fact get quite sophisticated. For example, students created a spotlight by cutting out a circle from construction paper and putting it on the overhead projector. Though students sometimes complain that seven minutes for practice is not enough, Oscar has found that the time control keeps students on task and encourages them to work effectively for this change-of-pace activity.

Torture

While this part of the day is still called Torture, Oscar and his students no longer believe that it *is* torture. Because his students originally groaned and complained, Oscar decided, "Rather than having kids moan and complain about explicit instruction, I'll call it what they think it is." During this period Oscar draws on strategies used in The Learning Edge, a curriculum developed by Bobbi Jentes Mason, as well as on ideas he has garnered from his mentor, Pam Smith. These include strategies for determining the author's intent, finding the controlling ideas in texts, and identifying the literary elements of a narrative.

Oscar recently used a Learning Edge strategy called "Framing a Narrative," adapted from Summerfield (1986). For this activity, Oscar chose a newspaper article about a school shooting, an article from *U.S. News and World Report,* and a photo from *Newsweek* of the boy who did the shooting. His students were especially interested in this topic because a hit list had been discovered at their own school. Oscar explains the background for this activity:

> Students were very upset about the school shootings in San Diego and the news that our own school had a student who had made a hit list of students and staff. Knowing how important it is to bring their world into the classroom as well as engaging students in reading and writing, I put together a text set [Short, Harste, and Burke 1996] of articles on the topic.

Oscar gave students time to read and discuss copies of the articles, working in small groups. The class also discussed the photo showing the shooter in the back of the police car with a facial expression that some students found interesting: he looked defiant and frightened at the same time. Oscar then showed them an outline of the steps for writing a position paper using an opinion-reasons-recommendation format (Berger 1996). Students were familiar with the format because they had used it with other readings.

The steps include giving an opinion about the shooting, writing it as a thesis statement. The students wrote their opinions, then listed reasons to support them. Last, they made a recommendation or offered a solution to the problem. Students completed this activity as a ten-minute quick write. Limiting the time for students to write in this way makes the task seem more manageable for students who struggle with writing in English.

Students then shared their writing in their small groups. Oscar asked for two volunteers from class to read what they had written to the whole class. Giving students a chance to share in a small group helps them build confidence for whole-class presentations. Next, the class brainstormed a list of people who had been affected by the shooting described in the articles. Students then chose one of the people and rewrote the news report as a narrative told from that person's point of view. Oscar again limited the time for writing to ten minutes. Finally, students shared their narratives with their small group.

One of Oscar's goals for this activity was to help students understand the difference between expository and narrative writing. He evaluated each position paper based on whether it had a thesis statement, supporting ideas, and a recommendation. The narratives, in contrast, needed a clear beginning, middle, and end, as well as some vivid sensory details to bring the story alive. Oscar encouraged students to put their narratives in their writing folders, and several students returned to these pieces later to develop them further.

The "Framing a Narrative" activity included all the constructs for effective instruction identified by Gersten and Jiménez (1994). Oscar challenged his students by giving them authentic pieces of writing that had not been adapted or simplified. He involved them in the activity by choosing articles about something that interested them. He promoted their success by scaffolding the instruction and mediating their learning in a number of ways. He had them work in collaborative groups, he limited the time for their writing to make the task less intimidating, he had them share in small groups, he provided a graphic organizer for their expository writing, and he led a brainstorming session to generate ideas for their narrative writing. By encouraging his students to express their opinions, Oscar showed he respected their diverse backgrounds.

During Torture, besides developing academic concepts such as the difference between expository and narrative texts and literary elements like point of view, Oscar also talks to students about the reading process and how readers effectively and efficiently use the three cueing systems as they learn to read. He teaches his students a little bit about miscue analysis and shows them strategies that will help them become better readers.

One such strategy is "Cooperative Cloze" (Goodman, Watson, Burke 1996). The teacher finds a good short story or content text and replaces some of the function words, like prepositions and conjunctions, and some of the content words, like nouns and verbs, with blanks. Students work in small groups to fill in the blanks. They talk through what words they think should go in the blanks. An important part of this strategy is for students to give reasons for their choices. Once the group is finished, they reread the text to see if they all agree on the word for each blank. Groups also have the right to agree to disagree. When all the groups are finished, the teacher can have them compare their stories with the original text. Students may find they did a better job than the author did. The value of this activity is in the process of discussing possible answers and defending the choices students make, not in getting the "right" answer. Students learn that during reading, they can use context cues to figure out what word fits logically in a sentence, even when the word is missing.

A way to extend this activity is to ask students which words were easy to fill in and which ones were hard. Generally, native English speakers will find the function words easier to decide on. There are only a few prepositions or conjunctions in our language, but many nouns and verbs. However, English language learners often find function words, especially prepositions, difficult to decide upon.

Students can discuss the clues they used to decide what kind of word should go in each blank. This activity helps them understand that the little function words play an important role in helping readers predict what is coming next. Readers also realize that they can often substitute different content words in a story without losing the meaning. Strategy lessons such as these provide the skills English learners need to tackle difficult academic texts. Oscar presents strategy lessons during both Torture time and the period of the day when the focus is on literature.

Literature

At different points in the year, Oscar's routine includes reading aloud from books chosen from the state-mandated list that the district has identified as core literature all students should read. Oscar has decided to read these books aloud because he knows they would be quite difficult for most of his students to read independently. He wants to involve them in interesting literature and help them build the academic English language register. He uses intonation, gestures, and visuals to help make the texts comprehensible to his English learners.

Listening to teachers read is one of the specific recommendations by Showers et al. (1998) for second-language students in middle and high school who are struggling with reading. Showers' research was carried out in a large high school where 40 percent of the students were Filipino, 30 percent African American, 20 percent Hispanic, and 10 percent Pacific Islander or Asian, including Laotian, Vietnamese, Thai, and Guamanian. The researchers identified features of reading programs that supported student reading success. They suggest active inquiry and the development of strategies that lead to independent reading. They found that students built vocabulary and improved their reading through reading and being read to in school and at home, and through the teaching of higher-order comprehension tasks such as identifying main ideas and interpreting what they read.

During the year Oscar read *A Child Called "It"* (Pelzer 1995), *The Circuit* (Jiménez 1997), and *Whirligig* (Fleischman 1998). *A Child Called "It"* is about a boy who is abused by his mother; *The Circuit* is a series of stories from the life of a migrant child; and *Whirligig* tells how the placement of whirligigs in the four corners of the country to atone for the death of a young girl changes the lives of many different people. These books encourage discussion and help students think, talk, and write to answer the year-long theme question "How do we deal with oppression?" Oscar has students consider different ways of responding to oppression: acquiescence, violence, or nonviolence. As they explore the big question, they also consider other questions: "Who is oppressed?" and "Who are the oppressors?"

Books such as the ones that Oscar reads to his students are rich sources for classroom discussions that can help students acquire academic language. One model for discussions that has proven especially successful with older English learners is the *instructional conversation* (Goldenberg 1991, 1992). Goldenberg points out that "true education—real teaching—involves helping students think, reason, comprehend and understand important ideas" (1992, 316). However, in many schools students are bombarded with mindless activities. This is especially true for many low-income minority students, who it is believed need frequent drill and repetition to learn. As Goldenberg observes, "instructional conversations—or good classroom discussions—are notable not only for their desirable attributes, but also for their rarity" (1992, 317).

Goldenberg has developed a model of an activity that is both instructional and conversational in nature. He identifies ten elements that characterize instructional conversations. The first five comprise the instructional component:

1. thematic focus
2. activation and use of background knowledge and relevant schemata
3. direct teaching of key skills or concepts related to the theme
4. promotion of more complex language and expression by the use of questions and requests for students to expand their answers
5. elicitation of bases for statements and positions (students have to give reasons and facts to support what they have said)

Elements six through ten are aimed at promoting good conversation:

6. fewer known-answer questions
7. responsivity to student contributions
8. connected discourse—the teacher helps link the ideas being generated
9. a challenging but nonthreatening atmosphere
10. general participation during which students take turns.

All these elements promote the development of lively academic conversations during which teachers can help students grapple with significant ideas.

Oscar engages students in the kinds of instructional conversations Goldenberg describes as they respond to literature. Oscar comments:

> I do a lot of think-alouds to model how one responds to literature and then engage students in classroom discussions. These whole-class conversations are crucial to the success of written responses.

He has students respond to his reading of the core texts in a variety of ways, such as writing in their literature logs. These logs serve as a reference during class discussions, and the responses allow students to apply the concepts about literature that Oscar is working on with them. Good classroom discussions provide the academic language students need when they begin to do more extended writing.

For example, when reading *A Child Called "It,"* Oscar specifically asked students to think about appropriate reader responses to literature. They were asked to respond to the following questions:

"What did you notice?"
"What did you question?"
"What did you feel?"
"What did you connect to?"

As Oscar reads their literature logs, he encourages his students to include answers to those questions in their responses. By providing specific questions, Oscar scaffolds the instruction and helps his students complete their assignments successfully.

Oscar gives his students a reading response rubric, developed by his mentor, Pam Smith, that they can use to evaluate their written responses to the literature he reads to them (Figure 5–3). The rubric makes the elements of a good response explicit: Students should retell the plot ("What did you notice?") and make personal connections to the text ("What did you question?" "What did you feel?" "What did you connect to?"). Students get the

Reading Response Rubric for an Open-Ended Response	
0	No response.
2.0	Inappropriate response, question not answered properly.
2.8	Retelling of the plot.
3.2	Retelling of the plot and your thoughts, feelings, or personal connections.
4.0	You discuss the reasons *why* something happened in the story or *why* a character acted the way he or she did; you compare and contrast characters, events, or the author's writing craft with other books you have read or movies or TV shows you have seen.
A bonus point will be awarded when you mention specific plots, characters, themes, or types of figurative language (similes, metaphors, etc.) that are comparable.	

FIGURE 5–3. *Reading Response Rubric (developed by Pam Smith)*

top score for telling why something happened, for comparing and contrasting, and for connecting this book to other books, movies, or TV shows.

Oscar has developed a form for record keeping and student self-evaluation. Students predict the grade their response will be given, then Oscar puts in his evaluation grade and makes comments. For example, in response to one student's log for *A Child Called "It,"* Oscar wrote, "Did a good job of telling what happened as well as what you thought. Include why you think David's mom acts that way." Through his comments, Oscar pushes his students to analyze what they have read or what he has read to them. Figure 5–4 shows one of the forms Oscar and a student used for *A Child Called "It."* This type of form helps keep students accountable and also gives them an opportunity to evaluate for themselves whether they are responding to their reading appropriately or not.

Writers Workshop and Closing

The final two parts of Oscar's routine are writers workshop and closing. Oscar's students do their longer pieces of writing and publishing during writers workshop. While they write, Oscar works with individuals and small groups giving minilessons on writing problems he notices students are experiencing.

Oscar bases his writers workshop on the format and suggestions of Graves (1994) and Atwell (1998). For example, he leads a status-of-the-class report at the beginning of the period. Many excellent ideas for minilessons of the kind Oscar teaches may be found in *Teaching Grammar in Context* (Weaver 1996). Teachers of older English learners can also gain valuable ideas for organizing writers workshop, providing students with feedback on their writing, improving students' accuracy, and assessing their writing from *Teaching ESL Composition: Purpose, Process, and Practice* (Ferris and Hedgcock 1998). This book contains an informative section on using technology to improve student writing.

Closing includes checking to be sure students understand their homework and that they write their assignments down on the calendars the school provides for that purpose. In the last few minutes, Oscar engages the students in various language-play activities that help them build vocabulary by making word associations and coming up with synonyms and antonyms.

Chapter	Anticipated Grade	Grade	Comments
1	2.8	2.8	You did a good job of telling me why something happened but not *why* you think it happened.
2	2.8	3.2	why do you think she changed? Explore those ideas.
3	2.8	2.8	José, don't repeat the story, I already read it. what did you think about it.
4	2.8	3.2	I can't believe how crazy she is. Why do you think she is like that?
5	2.8	3.2	Why doesn't the dad do something?
6	2.8	2.8	POOR kid thought the had changed.
7	3.2	3.2	It was selfish of the father but also he had turned into an alcoholic

FIGURE 5–4. *Student Evaluation Form*

Providing Scaffolds to Support Literacy Development

Throughout the day Oscar provides scaffolds for his students to help them become more proficient readers and writers. Providing scaffolded instruction is a key for success. Vygotsky (1981) explains that learning takes place when an adult or more capable peer asks questions, points out aspects of a problem, or makes suggestions working in a learner's *zone of proximal development* (ZPD)—the area between what a student can do independently and what he or she can do with some help. Good teaching attempts to target this zone by providing instruction that is slightly beyond a student's current capacity and also offering the help that a student needs to complete a challenging task.

Bruner (1985) referred to this kind of help as a *verbal scaffold*. A scaffold is an appropriate metaphor for this kind of assistance. A scaffold supports a building during its construction and then is taken down once the building is completed. Oscar continually provides support for his students so they can eventually work independently. He prods them to analyze their reading more carefully and to include more details in their responses. He asks students who have written a piece to expand on a certain point or to provide more information to support an argument. Oscar's questions and comments provide the scaffolding that allows his students to move toward becoming independent readers, writers, and thinkers.

Oscar provides different kinds of scaffolds for his students throughout the day, including reading aloud to them, having them write in literature logs, and giving them time for discussion to help them understand the reading they are doing and make connections to their personal lives, to other texts, and to the world. Many of the ideas Oscar uses to help students engage with literature in meaningful ways come from *Mosaic of Thought* (Keene and Zimmermann 1997). This book offers many examples of explicit instruction in the strategies used by proficient readers.

Oscar's approach to helping his English learners develop literacy is similar to the approach taken in a series of large-scale programs initiated by Elley (1998). He has found that students who are trying to learn to read English, especially those from third-world countries, lack resources, qualified teachers, and exposure to English. His research on literacy development all over the world, including in Fiji, Singapore, Sri Lanka, and South Africa (Elley 1991; Elley and Foster 1996; Elley and Mangubhai 1983), has shown that children succeed in becoming literate in English when their classrooms are flooded with large numbers of high-interest illustrated books and their teachers are shown simple methods of ensuring that the children interact regularly and productively with the books. Oscar's students are older than most of those in Elley's studies, but the formula for success is the same: access to books and support to make them comprehensible.

Sandra's Daily Routine

Like Oscar, Sandra has found that having classroom routines helps her students adjust to school and concentrate on learning to read, write, and problem solve. Her students must not only develop literacy in their first language, but also prepare themselves to succeed academically in English. Therefore, the daily routine includes many opportunities for students to develop literacy in their first and second languages while learning language through the study of academic content organized thematically.

Sandra's classroom is a learning community. All of her students work cooperatively with her and with each other as they read, write, and learn together. This community did not just happen. Sandra created it by drawing on what she knows about second-language acquisition, bilingual education, and literacy. Her expectations for her students are high, and she does not allow them to make excuses for not doing their work or not participating in activities. She provides many opportunities for her students to be in charge of their own learning, and they respond with hard work (Moran et al. 1993). Sandra insists on this: "When my kids do not do what they are supposed to do, I let them know. They know by my voice and a look from me if they aren't doing what they are supposed to be doing." Students respond positively because they realize that Sandra wants them to succeed academically. Both Sandra and her students understand that success will only come if everyone is fully engaged in meaningful learning.

The physical environment of the classroom promotes literacy and learning (Schifini 1997). Sandra's room is filled with professional and teacher-made posters, class-made books, student artwork, song and poetry charts, computers, a listening center, a math section, and a science corner. Everywhere there are books, including many literature and content books in card racks and in large, accessible open boxes. The classroom belongs to the students. On the first day of school, the students help Sandra set up the room, so they all know from the beginning where materials and books are kept. They also know that they all have the responsibility of taking care of what is there.

The room is set up for collaborative learning. There are three large tables in the middle of the room, and students are organized at the tables differently for different activities and projects. There is a round reading table in the back where Sandra or her classroom assistant can work with small groups. Along the wall behind that table are computers for student investigations and publishing, as well as lots of books in open boxes and on racks.

Science or social studies projects are usually displayed along the window wall. For example, when the class studied weather one year, the students made three aquariums—each with a lake fashioned out of clay, filled with water and greenery, and covered—to create condensation and rain in an experiment. During a study of Native Americans, the Native American habitats students had made were lined up for all to view and discuss. The wall opposite the windows has the listening center and song and poetry charts. In the front of the room, Sandra displays artwork, graphic organizers, brainstormed lists, and key books related to the theme study.

Materials are important to Sandra's teaching. Schifini (1997) suggests specifically that teachers have relevant, high-quality multicultural literature and information texts at various levels available to students. Sandra is very intentional about the books she chooses for her room. She has collected resources around themes, including theme packs that contain big books and small books at varying levels of difficulty. There are different theme packs with books on animals, plant growth, cultural celebrations, seasons, weather, and food (Rigby 2000/2001). She also uses the multicultural and bilingual *Saludos/Greetings* series (Rigby 1997) and various science big books that teach language and content, such as *Animal Clues* (Drew 1987a), *Caterpiller Diary* (Drew 1987b), *Mystery Monsters* (Drew 1987c), *Postcards from the Planets* (Drew 1988a), and *Somewhere in the Universe* (Drew 1988b).

Sandra is especially concerned that the texts she uses be accessible to her students and, when possible, culturally relevant. Since her students are older learners who need comprehensible texts to support their reading, she considers different factors as she makes her choices. She uses a checklist of characteristics of texts that support reading (Figure 5–5) to help her in her selections.

Like Oscar, Sandra uses picture books with older students. At one time, books with pictures were intended only for younger readers. In the last several years, however, publishers have produced a great many picture books

Characteristics of Texts That Support Reading
Materials for All Students
1. Are the materials authentic? Authentic materials are written to inform or entertain, not to teach a grammar point or a letter–sound correspondence.
2. Are the materials predictable? Prediction is based on the use of repetitive patterns, cumulative patterns, rhyme, alliteration, and rhythm. Books are also predictable if students have background knowledge about the concepts presented.
3. Is there a good text–picture match? A good match provides nonlinguistic visual cues? Is the placement of the pictures predictable?
4. Are the materials interesting, imaginative, or both? Interesting, imaginative texts engage students.
5. Do the situations and characters in the book represent the experiences and backgrounds of the students in the class? Culturally relevant texts engage students.
Additional Considerations for Older Students with Limited English Proficiency
1. Is the text limited?
2. Are the pictures, photographs, or other art appropriate for older students?
3. For content texts, are there clear labels, diagrams, graphs, maps, or other visuals?
4. Is the content age-level appropriate?

FIGURE 5–5.   *Characteristics of Texts That Support Reading*

for academic-content subjects that are appropriate for older students. In choosing picture books, teachers of older students must make sure that the illustrations are of older students or adults. Many of the content books use photographs. These books do not give older students the impression that they are being "babied." For example, Sandra uses a big-book version of the beautifully illustrated *The Tortilla Factory* (Paulsen 1995) when teaching about life cycles and the concept of how products move from the field to the table, and she uses *The Life of a Butterfly* (Drew 1989), a book full of close-up color photographs, to show the life cycle of butterflies.

Pictures are important context cues that make text more comprehensible. Many of the books that Sandra uses include maps, charts, graphs, and tables, which gives Sandra an opportunity to help her students learn how to read these graphics that are so much a part of content-area texts.

Sandra attempts to include many culturally relevant texts among the books she reads to and with her students. Students find these texts easier to read than others because the content, characters, and settings connect more closely to their lives. Sandra uses the cultural relevance rubric developed by A. Freeman (2000) as she chooses trade books for her students (Figure 5–6). While the classroom environment, including materials, is critical, it is the experiences that Sandra provides her students that ultimately lead them to success. Like Oscar, Sandra has developed a consistent classroom routine. This routine and the strategies and materials she uses during different parts of the day are described in the following sections. Figure 5–7 shows Sandra's routine.

Opening Activities

Sandra always begins her day with a whole-class discussion in which students volunteer any news they have to share. This time is important because it encourages the students to report their activities and present their ideas orally. They may share in Spanish or in English, though usually this discussion is in Spanish. Students appointed by Sandra on a rotating basis then direct the other opening activities. Different students take attendance and lead in a review of the calendar and date, which are displayed at the front of the room.

Another student then leads the whole group in a choral activity using posters, poetry, songs, or chants that are on the wall. Usually, these are related to the theme being studied. For example, during her immigrant unit, Sandra used posters including *American Stew, Immigrant's Chant, This Land Is Your Land,* and *A Nation of Immigrants* from the units "Coast to Coast" and "On the Way to the USA" in the program *Into English* (Hampton-Brown 1997).

The student directing the activity plays the poster's accompanying cassette and leads with a pointer as the other students read, sing, or chant together. Even though her students are fourth, fifth, and sixth graders, they enjoy this activity. The music is rhythmic and the students like reading and practicing

Cultural Relevance Rubric

1. Are the characters in the story like you and your family?

   Just like us . . . . Not at all like us

       4   3   2   1

2. Have you lived in or visited places like those in the story?

   Yes . . . . No

       4   3   2   1

3. Could this story take place this year?

   Yes . . . . No

       4   3   2   1

4. How close do you think the main characters are to you in age?

   Very close . . . . Not close at all

       4   3   2   1

5. Does the story have main characters who are boys (for boy readers)? Girls (for girl readers)?

   Yes . . . . No

       4   3   2   1

6. Do the characters talk like you and your family do?

   Yes . . . . No

       4   3   2   1

7. How often do you read stories like this one?

   Often . . . . Never

       4   3   2   1

8. Have you ever had an experience like one described in this story?

   Yes . . . . No

       4   3   2   1

FIGURE 5–6. *Cultural Relevance Rubric*

Daily Schedule Mrs. Mercuri's Class (4–6 Newcomers)	
8:10–8:30	• News of the day • Attendance • Calendar date • Song of the week
8:30–9:00	• Writers notebook
9:00–9:10	• Writers notebook sharing time
9:10–9:45	• Read aloud/shared reading • Phonemic awareness • (PE twice a week) (computer lab Friday)
9:45–10:15	• Recess
10:15–11:50	• Centers (students spend twenty minutes at each center) • Math • Listening center • Silent reading/library • Computer (editing or phonics) • Art • Guided reading (minilessons on critical thinking and comprehension strategies according to students' needs)
11:50–12:50	• Lunch
12:50–1:30	• Last rotation in centers
1:30–1:50	• D.E.A.R. time/Reader's theater
1:50–2:30	• Math
2:30–3:00	• Science
3:00–3:05	• Dismissal

FIGURE 5–7. *Sandra's Daily Schedule*

their English in this nonthreatening environment. Since the students read the chart or poster as they sing or chant, they develop literacy at the same time that they improve their intonation and pronunciation.

Writers Workshop

Sandra's students are emerging readers and writers in English. Many of them have limited or no literacy in their primary language. Therefore, Sandra scaffolds their writing time, especially at first. She spends around thirty minutes a day doing a language-experience activity related to the theme being studied. We've described how Sandra organized her students to develop a class immigrant story, and she often follows the same model for other theme studies: Working in small groups, her students brainstorm on a topic for their writing, using a graphic organizer, then they write a story as a small group. Next the whole class writes a story together, and groups share what they wrote. Students copy as Sandra writes on an overhead transparency. When the story is finished, students put it into a book and illustrate it for the class library.

Sometimes during writers workshop, students write on their own after Sandra provides some modeling, a form of support that a teacher can do with an individual, a small group, or an entire class. It is an intentional action by the teacher. Sandra models as she writes for her students before they write individually. For example, when the students were going to write about their families, Sandra wrote first about her own family, talking as she wrote:

> In the first sentence I indent and the first letter is a capital letter. My family has five people. Notice that I put a period at the end of the sentence. My husband's name is Alfredo. Notice that I have a capital letter at the beginning and for my husband's name.

As Sandra writes and talks, she models the kind of paragraph she wants her students to compose and the conventions she wants them to use. In this way, they develop English as they begin to express themselves in writing.

After the writing time, Sandra always has her students share what they have written. They may do this in small groups or with the whole class. Sharing writing in this way helps students develop a sense of audience. They realize that they need to include details, reasons, and descriptions so that their ideas will be communicated clearly.

One strategy that many teachers like Sandra have found helpful is "Read and Retell" (Brown and Cambourne 1987). Teachers begin by reading to and with their students a wide selection of texts from one genre. For example, they might choose science reports. Once students are familiar with the genre, teachers write the title of a new text on the board and have students predict the content and the vocabulary they might encounter. This helps activate students' background knowledge.

Next, the teacher gives each student a copy of the content text to read silently. With beginning English learners, the teacher might choose to read the text aloud as students follow along. After the reading, the students do a written retelling of the story without looking back at the text. They include as much of the original piece as they can remember.

Following the writing, students work in pairs or small groups. They read one another's written retellings and respond to them. They look to see what was included and what was left out. They notice the words the writer used. All of this helps students evaluate their ability to summarize different genres. Over time, their written retellings improve. Brown and Cambourne provide many good examples of texts of different types in their book *Read and Retell*. They also include many samples of student writing to show how students improve as they use this strategy.

Read-Aloud, Shared Reading, and Phonemic Awareness

After the class writes together, Sandra reads trade books or content books related to the theme. She often chooses a picture book in a big-book format because this allows her to conduct shared-reading sessions with the whole class. Shared reading is done using a predictable text that is big enough for the whole class to see. Sandra selects a few teaching points that the text lends itself to. First the class reads the story or content book together, or Sandra reads the story, having the students chime in during certain sections. It helps students who are just starting to read in English to hear a proficient reader pronounce the words.

Then Sandra might go back and use the book to teach a particular comprehension strategy. For example, she might cover up some words with sticky notes, then have students predict what words were covered and talk about the cues they used to make their predictions. Illustrated big books are well suited for shared reading. This activity provides a scaffold for students who may later choose to read a smaller version of the same book or another book on the same topic independently.

One reading comprehension strategy that many teachers have found to be useful is *reciprocal teaching*, which was developed by Palinscar (1986). During a reading session, the teacher asks a series of questions designed to help students make predictions, generate questions, give summaries, and clarify ideas. The teacher then instructs the students in how to ask these same kinds of questions, perhaps having one student predict what a story would be about by looking at the title. Once the teacher has worked with the students, the students practice these kinds of questions working in small groups. For example, before reading a section from a social studies text, one student could make predictions and a second could generate questions the students expect to answer by reading the selection. After the reading, a third student might summarize and the fourth could clarify the main ideas.

Over time, the students take on the role of teacher and ask other students the questions. Reciprocal teaching involves students in teaching one another. The process of modeling the questions, having individual students practice with the teacher, then having the students ask one another questions provides a kind of scaffolding that many English learners find helpful as they begin to read both literature and expository texts. Cooper (1999) has developed the *Soar to Success* reading series for middle school students, which makes extensive use of reciprocal teaching. The series contains a number of books at different levels of difficulty that are attractive, engaging, and interesting. Teachers of older English learners have found these materials to be extremely useful.

Sandra's reading time is often followed by discussion or an activity related to the theme to support students' comprehension, build vocabulary, and develop concepts. During the immigrant theme, for example, students compared two of the Cinderella books they had read. During the From the Field to the Table theme, Sandra read literature books about different dishes and students in groups made posters that showed the ingredients of a dish, where it came from, and how to prepare the dish.

Because the school district requires that some time be spent on phonemic awareness, Sandra specifically helps her students with English and spelling through various alphabet- and vocabulary-building activities during this period. For each letter of the alphabet, the students brainstorm words that are related to the theme study (see Figure 4–5, the ABC chart for the immigrant unit). They also make alphabet books and talk about words and other conventions of English sentence structure and punctuation.

Centers

Many different activities take place during centers. Sandra has her students do guided reading with her during this time. Guided reading is carried out with small homogeneous groups of readers. Students with similar levels of English reading proficiency read with Sandra in groups of four or five. Usually they start by rereading some familiar books individually. Students choose these books from a set that Sandra has selected for this group.

After about ten minutes, Sandra goes around and asks different students in the group to read aloud at the point where they are. This gives her an opportunity to evaluate the student's progress in reading different kinds of texts. Then she introduces a new book, showing the cover and asking what the students think the book will be about. After they make predictions, Sandra does a "picture walk" through the book. As she turns the pages, she points to different pictures and talks with the students about what they see. She makes a point of using some of the vocabulary that appears in the text.

Then each student gets a copy of the book, and they read it aloud together as a choral reading. If Sandra is working with a newcomer group with very limited literacy, she may first read the book to the students and have them track the words as she reads, then have the students read it with her, tracking as they read. Once the story is finished, they discuss it. Next Sandra presents a teaching point for the small group. For example, she might lead a discussion about what to do when they come to a word they don't know.

Guided reading offers teachers the opportunity to work closely with students who are at roughly equivalent proficiency levels in reading. This procedure, which was originally used with younger students, has proven effective with older beginning readers as long as the content of the materials is suitable for the age of the readers. Like shared reading, guided reading allows teachers to scaffold instruction and provide the support that beginning readers at any age need.

While Sandra works with small groups, other students use the computers to look up information for research or write and edit reports of their projects. During this time students also listen to books at the listening center, do silent reading in the library, or work on art projects related to the theme. Groups of students rotate through different activities during center time, which extends into the period following lunch.

DEAR Time, Reader's Theatre, Math, and Science

DEAR (Drop Everything And Read) is a favorite time for all Sandra's students. Since she has so many books on various topics written at different levels of difficulty, all her students can find something to read. Often, students choose to read books Sandra has read to them, but at other times they choose books that interest them or that they are using for research. Since Sandra puts out a large selection of books related to the theme being studied, DEAR time offers students the chance to continue their theme study as they read.

Reader's theatre is not something that is done every day, but several times during the year Sandra and her students work on a play they have written connected to their language-experience writing and the theme they are studying. For example, when studying the question "Why is agriculture important?" the students studied farm animals. Then they wrote together a story titled "The Hen and the Little Kernel." With the student teacher, who had minored in drama in college, they converted the story into a play, made props and puppets, and performed their puppet show for the younger students.

This activity combined reading, writing, speaking, and listening. It was an integral part of the students' theme study and extended the concepts they were developing. Changing a story into a play helps students begin to understand the conventions of different genres. For example, the dialogue in a story is indicated by quotation marks, but in a play script no quotation marks are used. Performing the reader's theater gave students practice in both reading and speaking. Sandra's students always enjoy this kind of activity, so she includes it whenever she can.

Sandra also integrates math and science content into her themes. During the agriculture theme, for example, students measured and graphed the plant growth of seeds in pocket gardens, potato eyes, and carrot roots. They carried out an experiment studying how liquids travel through plants, placing celery stalks in glasses of water that contained different food colors. Over several days they observed what happened as the celery absorbed the colored water, recording the results in a journal and making hypotheses about what was happening.

At the end of the day, Sandra gathers her students, reviews their homework assignments, answers any last questions, and dismisses them. Students in her class are engaged throughout the day in a series of challenging activities. Sandra focuses especially on their literacy development and organizes her curriculum around a series of related themes. Because she provides support and also follows a predictable routine each day, her students make remarkable progress in developing both academic English and subject-area knowledge and skills.

Conclusion

Both Oscar and Sandra have established routines for their students. By creating these predictable structures, they free their students to concentrate on academic content learning. During each day, these teachers consciously employ a number of scaffolds to support student learning, and they use a variety of strategies to involve their students and to help them succeed. Both teachers have collected large classroom libraries with materials organized around the themes they teach. This gives all their students access to appropriate books and magazines. Oscar and Sandra's students are struggling older English learners, but because their teachers follow practices that are consistent with the keys for success, the students have started to close the achievement gap as they have begun to build confidence in themselves, to value school, and to value themselves as capable learners.

Professional Extensions

1. Write down your own daily classroom routine or that of a teacher you observe. Think through each of the parts of the routine and explain the rationale behind that portion of the day. Does the routine include the constructs for effective instruction identified by Gersten and Jiménez?
2. Oscar and Sandra make sure that their students have access to many reading resources. Look at your own classroom or the classroom of someone you observe and describe the resources available to the students. As an alternative, take photos of the classroom and be prepared to describe the resources they show.
3. Access to books is a key to school success for older learners. Survey your students or a class of students with older LFS students or LTELs to find out the following:

♦ how many have public library cards

♦ how many live within walking distance to a library

♦ how many live in a home where the newspaper is delivered daily

♦ how many read books outside of those assigned in school

♦ what they read outside of school (magazines, newspapers, books)

♦ how much they read outside of school.

Looking at the results, what are some of your conclusions?

4. Both Sandra and Oscar scaffold instruction for their students in various ways. Look back over the chapter and choose two strategies that you could use with students. Explain how you would apply the strategies within a content area related to a theme you are teaching or might teach.

5. The choice of appropriate reading materials is critical for English learners. Put together a text set of books, articles, or a combination of the two that you could use during a theme study in your content area. Explain why you chose those readings, referring to the list in Figure 5–5. How would you have students respond to the texts? Include at least one graphic organizer you would use to help students access the content of the readings.

6. If you use literature in your class and your students are older, have them evaluate their reading using the cultural relevance rubric in Figure 5–6. Discuss the results with them. Describe the results of this activity.

Using the Four Keys to Close the Achievement Gap

I Am Mireya

I am Mireya
My roots come from Mexico
I am an immigrant to America
My blood has survived the wars in Mexico
My people encourage Mexican traditions to their familys and
    children

I am Mireya
I am confused by the world and my future
It is like a roller coaster ride
That goes and goes but when it brakes it dies,

It is like your goals die too.
I weep when I see my friends taking drugs,
Knowing that they are hurting themselves, family, and even friends.

I am Mireya
I strive to be a friend you can trust,
And to always know I can live my life how I want
Opening the doors to an education and a better life
I will live out this dream
I am Mireya

These excerpts from Mireya's poem tell us about her past, her present, and her future. The poem was part of a three-layered Tree of Life project Grace and her students completed late in the year. It is modeled after the poem "I Am Joaquin" (González 1993), which Grace and her students read and discussed together. The Tree of Life project culminates a yearlong theme that answers such questions as "Who are we?" "Where have we come from?" and "Who are the people who influenced us?"

In Chapter 2 we explained how Mireya, a long-term English learner, had been known as a troublemaker and had struggled academically before entering Grace's eighth-grade language arts class. However, Grace was encouraged when she read Mireya's response to an early assignment. When students start in her class, Grace asks them to write a letter to her in which they answer specific questions, shown in Figure 6–1.

Excerpts from Mireya's letter show both discouragement and hope.

Dear Ms. Klassen

The important thing for me is pass 8th grade. Show my family I culd pass this year . . . Well Ms. Klassen I will tell you the true I never like reading or write. That is my worst subject. But I want to be better on those two things. I hope you could help me. Last year I was a truble maker but I wont be the way any more. I want to learn. I just need more help . . . .

Make my daddys dream come true. Pass 8th grade this year. Be better on writing, reading & splling. I think that be the end of the year I'll be better. I think I culd make it no matter what. I hope you could help me.

Grace's goal is to do what Mireya asks for. During the year Grace and her students do a great deal of reading of literature, writing, and oral sharing, and this enables them to develop the academic competence they need.

•	What is important to you?
•	What are your interests outside of school?
•	How do you feel about books and reading?
•	What are your concerns and worries about this class?
•	What are your goals in this class?
•	How will you achieve your goals?
•	What are your strengths and talents?
•	What are your study habits like?
•	What is your most important goal?

FIGURE 6–1. *Questions for Letter to Teacher*

Grace works closely with the social studies teacher in planning and orga-
nizing around themes to integrate literature and history. For social studies,
U.S. history is covered in the eighth grade and the stories of diversity that
Grace uses in language arts are a natural complement to the history focus.

Reading and Responding

Grace and her students begin the year by reading novels, short stories, and
poems to get at the question "Who are we?" To scaffold the reading for her
English learners, Grace reads many picture books, articles, and poems
aloud. Students follow along in their own copies. This allows the students
to acquire academic English. They hear correct pronunciation and intonation. For struggling readers, hearing a story or poem read by a competent
reader is a first step to enjoying good books. After Grace reads, she has students respond with a quick write. Students share their written responses in
small groups and then report back to the whole class. Grace follows this
reading routine consistently. She finds it helps increase student comprehension. Knowing they will write, share, and report back also increases their attention as Grace reads.

They read from *Living up the Street* (Soto 1992), which contains excerpts
about the lives of Hispanics in California's central valley, where Grace's
students live. They also read about young migrant workers in *The Circuit*

(Jiménez 1997) and about the experiences of other Hispanics in *The House on Mango Street* (Cisneros 1984). In their written responses, the students connect the readings to their own lives in a variety of ways.

One of the first formal writing assignments Grace gives is an *autobiopoem*—an autobiographical poem. The fixed format for this form offers struggling writers a scaffold. It also helps students begin to use descriptive words, specific nouns, and verbs intentionally. The autobiopoem assignment engages Grace's reluctant writers because it includes topics they are interested in: their likes, their feelings, their needs, and their hopes and dreams. Figure 6–2 shows the outline of one autobiopoem model (Freeman and Freeman 1998a).

This assignment helps prepare students to write a personal memoir. For the memoir students must select one memory and describe it in detail. Readings from Soto, Jiménez, and Cisneros provide models. Grace's students enjoy writing about themselves, and Grace builds assignments that support their efforts to express themselves in English.

Autobiopoem	
Follow these instructions and you will see that you are a poet:	
Line 1:	Write your first name.
Line 2:	Write four adjectives that describe you.
Line 3:	Son/daughter of . . . or brother/sister of . . .
Line 4:	Who feels (three words that describe your emotions)
Line 5:	Who finds happiness in (three things)
Line 6:	Who needs (three things)
Line 7:	Who gives (three things)
Line 8:	Who is afraid of (three things)
Line 9:	Who would like to (three things)
Line 10:	Who likes to wear (three colors or things)
Line 11:	Resident of (city, street, road)
Line 12:	Write your last name

FIGURE 6–2. *Autobiopoem*

Grace and her students go through a shared process to edit all their writing. It begins with a brainstorming session to decide what should be included in the writing piece. Grace writes the students' suggestions on an overhead projector transparency, putting content suggestions on the left side and suggestions for the mechanics of writing on the right. Content suggestions include characteristics of the genre the students will be writing. This helps student begin to understand differences between different genres, such as a memoir and a poem. Under mechanics, Grace lists the details of conventional writing that students need to look at, including spelling, punctuation, indentation, and so on. In this way, students follow the school district's requirements for writing and at the same time begin to internalize what they should look for in editing their work. Grace finds that students always make more suggestions than are reasonable to work with, so she takes their ideas, pares the list down, and makes copies of the shortened list for students to use.

The editing process involves reading each piece three times. The first reading is to get the meaning. The second reading focuses specifically on the content. The third reading is a check of the mechanics. When they receive the lists, students first look at their own writing and edit following the guidelines they have come up with. Students work in pairs. After the writer of the piece has edited to his or her satisfaction, using the editing sheet, the partner reads the piece three times and makes notes on the draft and the editing sheet in a different color of pen. After each student has read the partner's piece, the two sit down together and go over the suggestions and the comments.

Finally, the writer edits again and goes to a final draft, unless he or she does not feel comfortable with the piece and wants to repeat the process. Final drafts are usually published. The memoirs, for example, are illustrated and put into a book for the classroom library. These student memoirs become some of the most frequently read texts in the classroom.

The Tree of Life Project

The autobiopoems and memoirs serve as background for students to produce their Tree of Life projects. The three parts of this project include writing a poem, like Mireya's "I Am Mireya," modeled after "I Am Joaquin";

creating a Road of Life section, and, finally, writing a Reflection on Heritage. These are all put onto three large circular pieces of construction paper about twelve inches in diameter. The three circles are attached in the middle with a brad so they can be rotated. Students cut a triangle out of the top circle, so that one eighth of the second circle is visible. The writing on the bottom circle faces in the opposite direction. This construction allows all three circles to be read. Students not only write for this project but also decorate the project with great care.

On the top circle students print their three-stanza "I Am . . ." poems, representing the past, the present, and the future. On the second circle students put the Road of Life portion of the project. For this part, students choose eight significant events in their lives to write up in short sections so that each will fit onto an eighth of the circle. In one section Mireya wrote

> 1986 I was born. I was born on a sidewalk. In Sanbernardino outside my house. My mother was so happy but not that happy. She wasn't with my dad no more. She was sad but happy. She was with my aunt. My aunt name me Mireya. Everyone in the house was in love with me. I was the only baby born in the house.

Mireya finished this and every triangle she wrote with a symbolic drawing. This drawing showed a pregnant woman saying, "Help, I am having a baby." In other triangles Mireya wrote about her happy and painful memories: of kindergarten and a friend she made who is still her best friend, of taking care of a baby sister when her parents worked, of being made fun of because she had physically matured sooner than other girls, of working when she was sixteen so her mother wouldn't have to work so hard.

The last circle of the Tree of Life Project is attached to the back of the others. For this, students think of artifacts that represent their heritage and write about them. Mireya wrote about a necklace her grandmother had given her mother when she was married in the church, of a family dish that everyone loves to eat, of advice her grandfather gave her, and of a poem, "Don't Ever Give Up Your Dreams," that her uncle wrote to her the day before he died when she was only thirteen. The last line reads, "Sometimes you may even wonder if it's really worth it. But I have confidence in you and I know you'll make it if you try." Mireya wrote the poem onto the circle and added, "He told me don't ever forget this poem. I know it's true!"

Follow Your Dreams

One wonders if this poem was part of what gave Mireya the strength and determination to change her ways in Grace's class. During the middle of the year, the theme that students work on has an inner focus, and students begin to seriously consider their rights, their strengths, and their potential. In this part of the year the big questions become "What are our values?" and "Where are we going?"

Students do a self-study connected to their values and interests. They take a personal-interest inventory and also study modern-day problems, problems that so many of them have seen in their lives, including abuse, divorce, and drug addiction. A culminating project is a letter they write to the person who will be their high school counselor next year. Mireya's typed letter tells about the things she is good at: "I am very good at sports. I like to play sports a lot." It shows a variety of interests: "I was in choir in 6th and 7th grade too. This year I decided to try something else like art. But I really like singing." It shows she has pride in her bilingualism: "Some time I even write songs in Spanish." And it relates her pleasure at the results of the interest survey she took: "Poet was in there too and reporter. I talk a lot and my mother tells me I should be a reporter." Mireya concluded her letter by telling how people are surprised at the changes they see in her:

> That's why when they ask me what happen to you? I proudly say I am how really I am and how I want to be. So I tell all my friends never give up their dreams and to try all they can and you will see you could.

Mireya followed her uncle's advice and did not give up her dreams. She still has some work to do to achieve the academic competence she needs to succeed for long-term education. However, she has made great progress in a year. Grace and the curriculum were key to Mireya's turnaround. Grace engaged Mireya in challenging activities that connected to Mireya personally. She helped her develop academic English, and she certainly created a confident learner. In some summary comments about Mireya, Grace wrote the following:

> She still struggles in reading and writing, and she didn't see herself as "good" in language arts. She thought she was "dumb" in August of 2000. Yet, in eighth grade she fell in love with poetry / She loves Langston Hughes' poetry, music, sports, dancing and art. Her confidence has soared!

Keys to Closing the Gap

Grace is an effective teacher. Faced with students like Mireya, she develops a meaningful curriculum and employs strategies to build Mireya's confidence and competence. Grace is the kind of proactive teacher that Purcell-Gates (1995) says our schools need:

> Proactive teachers do not simply wring their hands when confronted with failure to learn. They do not simply shake their heads and refer unsuccessful children out to "specialists." They do not simply blame the children themselves for failure. Nor do they simply blame the children's parents or cultures. Acknowledging complexity, proactive teachers *do* something for each child; they take action based on their knowledge of culture, cognition, and schooling. (194)

Grace fits the description of a proactive teacher. She uses her knowledge of "culture, cognition, and schooling" as she plans her lessons. Throughout this book, we have reviewed the research and the theoretical concepts that inform effective teaching. We have shown how teachers like Grace, Oscar, and Sandra put the theory into practice.

In Chapter 1 we identified four keys that lead to successful teaching (Figure 1–2). In Chapter 3 we showed how these keys are consistent with a large body of research about older English learners. In the following sections we review each of the four keys and show how they can be implemented. While there are no easy solutions to the challenge of closing the achievement gap for struggling older English learners, these four keys can be used to teach them successfully.

Key 1: Engage Students in Challenging, Theme-Based Curriculum to Develop Academic Concepts

A recurrent research recommendation is that teachers must challenge students. Too often, English learners have been relegated to a skill-and-drill curriculum. In some schools, even when second-language students have been given access to technology, they sit in front of computers that give them endless spelling lists or math problems. What these students need is the chance to engage with big ideas that push their thinking. Just because these students can't speak English well doesn't mean they can't think.

The projects Grace has developed with her students challenge them to think. These struggling English learners write poems, like Mireya's "I Am

Mireya," that follow literary models. They write responses to novels and then closely edit one another's work. They write memoirs following the models of published authors. All of this instruction occurs within a theme study organized around big questions. Theme-based curriculum is important for English learners because it provides continuity for their instruction.

Challenging students, setting high standards, is a key to helping students succeed. However, unless teachers carefully scaffold their instruction, the students may feel overwhelmed and simply give up. Grace is careful to make the English input comprehensible, and she provides many supports to help students develop academic concepts. She reads to them. She has them respond with quick writes and share in small groups and whole-class discussions. All these activities, organized around a central theme, help students develop the language and concepts they need for their writing. Grace also gives them clear guidelines for editing their work. Students engage in projects like the Tree of Life, and for each step, Grace gives them models and clear directions. All of this scaffolded instruction mediates their learning and leads them to success.

Grace's goal is to help students develop academic concepts and the academic register of English. Since she is a language arts teacher, she presents the scientific concepts from her discipline. Vygotsky (1962) defined *scientific concepts* as the abstract terms that are used to show logical relationships. To teach scientific concepts, Grace builds on the spontaneous concepts her students have developed. For example, her students know from personal experience something about the differences among people, including how some are honest and hardworking while others are not. As they read literature, Grace helps them develop related scientific concepts to analyze literary characters and the devices that authors use to develop character in a piece of literature. They also learn about other concepts, like foreshadowing and flashbacks. On their editing sheets, they list the characteristics of each genre they study. Grace also coordinates with the social studies teacher to reinforce concepts from that discipline. Grace's approach has helped long-term English learners like Mireya begin to develop the scientific concepts and academic language they need to succeed in high school.

Key 2: Draw on Students' Background— ### Their Experiences, Cultures, and Languages

Grace does not speak Spanish, but she has learned a great deal about the cultural background of her students. Her projects all build on her students' experiences and cultural heritage. They write autobiopoems and memoirs. The novels, short stories, and poems Grace reads to them are culturally relevant. They read literature by Hispanic authors. Grace's curriculum connects to the lives of her students and draws them in to academic study by building on what they bring to the classroom.

Many of Grace's students are what Ogbu (1991) has identified as *involuntary minorities*. Often long-term English learners (LTELs) display the characteristics of involuntary minority groups. These groups are aware of their position in the social hierarchy, and they may develop ways to resist the discriminatory treatment they receive. Mireya admits she was a "truble maker" in the past, but says "I wont be the way any more. I want to learn." She wants to make her "daddys dream come true. Pass 8th grade this year." With Grace's help, she is accomplishing that goal.

LTELs like Mireya who are involuntary minorities need the kind of transformative intercultural curriculum that Grace offers to overcome negative attitudes they may have developed toward mainstream institutions such as schools. Grace plans activities that draw on students' cultural heritage. The Tree of Life project is designed to answer the big questions "Who are we?" "Where have we come from?" and "Who are the people who influenced us?"

It is important for Grace's students to examine these questions because, like other involuntary minorities, they suffer from cultural ambivalence. They may not have a clear conception of their own cultural heritage, yet clearly they are not part of U.S. mainstream culture. Without an understanding of their past, it is difficult for them to envision their future. Projects like the Tree of Life help them connect with their past so that they can follow their dreams and move more confidently into the future.

School curriculum should draw on all students' experiences, cultures, and languages. For new arrivals with limited formal schooling (LFS), like Sandra's students, it is equally important to build on what they bring to school. LFS students share the characteristics of what Ogbu calls *immigrant minorities*. They do know who they are. Many of them develop a dual frame of reference. They are not culturally ambivalent. Instead, they can act, dress, and speak one way in school and a different way at home.

What is important for working with LFS students is to tap into their language and cultural resources. Sandra does this by choosing theme studies that connect to their lives, such as her units on agriculture and immigrants. Sandra also uses the preview/view/review technique to draw on her students' primary language strengths. She always introduces new concepts in their first language and then conducts a primary language review. Sandra knows that students can learn new concepts most easily in their first language. Knowledge gained in one language then transfers to a second language, according to Cummins' *interdependence* hypothesis. By providing primary language instruction, Sandra draws on her students' experiences, cultures, and languages to help them develop academic concepts and academic language.

Key 3: Organize Collaborative Activities and Scaffold Instruction to Build Students' Academic English Proficiency

Language and thinking are closely related. School success depends on the development of scientific concepts. Each academic discipline is based on a number of such concepts. Studying the discipline involves gaining the knowledge of the concepts and the language needed to talk about the concepts.

Vygotsky (1978) has shown that students develop new concepts by working with an adult or a more capable peer who asks questions or points out aspects of a problem. Instruction that is within a student's *zone of proximal development* (ZPD), the area just beyond the student's current level of proficiency, serves as a scaffold to mediate learning. What students can first do with help, they can later do independently. This is why it is so important for teachers to organize learning activities so that students can work together collaboratively.

Working together, students can begin to build academic English proficiency. Cummins (1981) differentiates between *conversational language*, used to talk or write about everyday events, and *academic language*, used for classroom discourse. Conversational language is context-embedded and cognitively undemanding. In contrast, academic language is used to talk about different content-area subjects. It is the literacy-based language of the classroom. Academic language is both context-reduced and cognitively demanding. Teachers build students' academic English proficiency by helping them develop both the concepts and the academic language used to express those concepts.

Grace uses a number of strategies to help her students develop academic proficiency. She scaffolds instruction as she reads aloud or has students edit their written work. She works collaboratively with her students and then has them work in small groups or pairs. Oscar and Sandra use similar strategies to help their students develop academic English.

School success depends on the development of academic language proficiency, but as Cummins (2000) and other researchers, including Collier (1992) have shown, this takes time, usually from five to nine years. Older students have limited time. One year they might have an excellent teacher—like Sandra, Oscar, or Grace—who understands "culture, cognition, and language" and can organize collaborative instruction to move their students toward proficiency. But the next year, the instruction may be less effective. For that reason, school systems need to implement comprehensive programs that offer continued support for older English learners and give them a real chance to succeed.

Key 4: Create Confident Students Who Value School and Value Themselves as Learners

The fourth key to success is to create confident learners. Most older English learners, whether they are LTEL or LFS students, are not confident. School is either a place where they have experienced consistent failure or it is a new, strange world. Many older English learners really don't know what they are supposed to do in school because they haven't been socialized into the culture of schools. It is not that they don't want to learn, it's that they aren't sure where to start.

Teachers like Grace build curriculum around themes based on questions that are important to students and include many activities, like the autobiopoem, that draw on students' background as a way of making school a more welcoming and relevant place. Thematic instruction makes the school day more predictable. Students have the big picture, so they can make sense of the details more easily. Further, Grace employs a number of strategies to scaffold instruction so her students can succeed and start to build confidence. As they become more confident, her students come to value school and to value themselves as learners.

Effective teachers establish regular routines. Oscar and Sandra's students know what is expected each day. Having a consistent routine teaches students how schools work. Having a regular routine frees students to focus on the academic concepts. Within their routines, Oscar, Sandra, and Grace use various strategies to mediate their students' learning. They use these strategies on a regular basis, so students learn how to do quick writes, how to respond to readings, and how to edit their papers. In the process they become more confident and competent. They start to value school and to value themselves as learners.

The four keys to success we have discussed in this section are good reminders of what constitutes effective instruction for struggling older English learners. All four are consistent with the research on effective schooling, and all four draw on important theoretical constructs. When teachers follow these guidelines, they increase the chance for success for their older English learners, and, in fact, they increase the chance for success for all their students.

Older English learners, both long-term English learners and students with limited formal schooling, need effective instruction to succeed in school. We have introduced readers to many of these students, the research and theory that should guide their instruction, and teachers who have worked effectively with these students. We conclude this book with one more example, an extended description of an effective teacher. We chose Grace's theme study because it exemplifies the keys to success that help older English learners close the achievement gap.

El Día de los Muertos

I will never forget our *el Día de los Muertos* celebration in Room 1! I began our celebration by honoring my grandmother, Martha. It was amazing to feel the bond of human empathy as I told a funny remembrance and a poignant moment, too. After I shared my memory, the class honored her by saying her name out loud in unison, and my heart soared. As each class member followed in turn, an incredible support network bloomed. Students voluntarily joined friends shedding tears to show they were not alone. It was stunning. I never expected, could not have planned for such a day. The impact lingered all year. It set a tone for openness and trust that surpassed every other year of teaching.

Grace's words show the power of a theme study that helps students connect to their roots and honor who they are. This celebration that she initiated with her eighth graders during their larger Developing the Promise of Democracy theme study did not just happen. It took thought, preparation, and sensitivity to organize.

Background: El Día de los Muertos
(The Day of the Dead) Celebration

Several years ago when she was working with Lorena, one of her eighth graders, Grace became aware of the Mexican tradition of honoring the dead on November 1, All Saints' Day. For her individual project within the Developing the Promise of Democracy theme, Lorena had chosen to investigate Mexican folkways. She was reading Mexican authors, Mexican folktales, and Mexican history. At the end of her personal investigation, Lorena reported what she had learned about the traditions of Mexicans in this country and also proudly described many beliefs and traditions from her region of Oaxaca in southern Mexico.

After class that day, Lorena shared with Grace pictures of her family's celebration of the Day of the Dead, explaining to her the special rituals and foods they enjoyed together. Grace then showed Lorena a giant poster of a purple skeleton that came with a book a friend had given her, *Mexico: The Day of the Dead* (Sayer 1993). Lorena took the book home to share with her family.

Three years later, Grace was reminded of this experience when she came upon another book about the celebration, *The Skeleton at the Feast: The Day of the Dead in Mexico* (Carmichael and Sayer 1997). It occurred to Grace that she could include a comparative study of Halloween and *el Día de los Muertos* as part of their yearlong theme study. She had in mind that she would share a remembrance of her own grandmother, and, recalling the pictures Lorena had shown her years before of the family at the table, she searched for and found an old-fashioned cardboard picture frame for her grandmother's picture. During this same time she came home one day to find a journal article about the power of remembering loved ones attached to an invitation from a neighbor to attend a celebration of *el Día de los Muertos*. That experience with neighbors and friends became the foundation for Grace's classroom celebration.

Launching the Theme

Grace decided to start the Day of the Dead theme right after she and her students returned to school after a two-week fall break. During the first quarter Grace's students had completed their autobiopoems and their memoirs; read stories from authors from the central valley of California; and moved on to a study of Native American customs, legends, and values. From that study of Native Americans and their influence, Grace's classes and the social studies classes prepared to examine the influences of European settlers and other immigrants. The focus of this study would be early American folklore, including tall tales, legends, folkways, superstitions, and folk crafts.

Since students returned from their break right before Halloween, Grace decided it was the perfect time for a comparative study of Halloween and *el Día de los Muertos*. To begin, Grace shared a short reading she had found about the Mexican festival on a greeting card that emphasized the idea that before we can understand where we are going, it is important for us to understand where we have been. She also read a short poem from *Cool Salsa: Bilingual Poems on Growing Up Latino in the United States*, titled "Día de los Muertos" (Delgado 1994), and the book *Pablo Remembers: The Fiesta of the Day of the Dead* (Diaz 1993). This led to the big questions "Who are we and where have we been?" and "Who are the people who have influenced us?"

Developing the Theme

After the readings, Grace asked her students to think about the differences between the Mexican celebration and Halloween. Her students moved to small groups to brainstorm the differences. Next, the groups read articles about the two celebrations and filled in information on a graphic organizer Grace provided. Then, each small group reported their results to the rest of the class. As each group reported, their classmates added details to their own charts. Figure 6–3 shows the graphic organizer the students used. This activity helped build background knowledge.

Grace talked to the students about the decoration of the Day of the Dead *ofrenda* (offering table). The class discussed how the traditional tables for the celebration are decorated with photographs of loved ones who have died and with poetry, stories, food, candles, and flowers. Students volunteered to bring items to decorate their classroom table for the day of the celebration. They also planned to write poems, stories, and memoirs to put on the table.

To prepare for the writing, students read poems, narratives, and memoirs by various authors about special people in their lives. In their small groups, students read aloud these texts, many of which were written by Hispanic authors. Then group members responded by doing quick writes followed by a discussion. During a quick write, students write for one or two minutes, giving their reactions to something without worrying about spelling or grammar. Students can then use the ideas they generate as a basis for discussion and further writing. After the students had responded to the readings in their small groups, Grace led a whole-class discussion to summarize the key ideas from the readings. Figure 6–4 lists the books Grace used in this activity.

Halloween	El Día de los Muertos
Origin (notes and sketch)	Origin (notes and sketch)
Origin (notes and sketch)	Preparation (notes and sketch)
Origin (notes and sketch)	Activities (notes and sketch)
Custom (notes and sketch)	Procession (notes and sketch)

Custom (notes and sketch)	• Highlight similarities
	• Explain differences in purpose:
	    — The purpose of Halloween is . . .
	    — The purpose of *el Día de los Muertos* is . . .

Custom (notes and sketch)	Who can you honor at our celebration on_____?

FIGURE 6–3. *Comparison Graphic Organizer*

Ada, A. F. 1997. *Gathering the Sun.* New York: Lothrop, Lee & Shepard Books.

Atkins, B. 1997. *Voices from the Fields.* New York: Little, Brown.

Cisneros, S. 1984. "Born Bad." In *House on Mango Street.* New York: Lothrop, Lee & Shepard Books.

————. 1984. "Papa Who Wakes Up Tired in the Night." In *House on Mango Street.* New York: Lothrop, Lee & Shepard Books.

Delgado, A. 1994. "Día de los Muertos." In *Cool Salsa: Bilingual Poems on Growing Up Latino in the United States,* edited by L. Carlson. New York: Henry Holt and Co.

Jiménez, F. 1997. "Death Forgiven." In *The Circuit: Stories from the Life of a Migrant Child.* Albuquerque: University of New Mexico Press.

Landa, V. 1996. "To Live and Die Is to Be Remembered." *San Antonio Express News,* 3 November, 7.

Myers, W. D. 1993. "History of My People." In *Soul Looks Back in Wonder,* edited by T. Feelings. New York: Dial Books.

Okantah, M. 1993. "Window Morning." In *Soul Looks Back in Wonder,* edited by T. Feelings. New York: Dial Books.

Quiroz, C. 1994. "Memories of Uncle Pety." In *Cool Salsa: Bilingual Poems on Growing Up Latino in the United States,* edited by L. Carlson. New York: Henry Holt and Co.

Rylant, C., and E. Walker. 1993. "Shoes." In *Something Permanent.* New York: Harcourt Brace and Co.

FIGURE 6–4. *Bibliography of Memory Books*

This reading built background for the students' writing. Grace gave them specific guidelines for different types of writing. Students prepared an epitaph and a memorial for the person they decided to commemorate. Some students also prepared a *calacas* scene, a shadow box with a clay skeleton of the deceased engaged in a favorite activity. Figure 6–5 shows the guidelines Grace provided and Figure 6–6 is the epitaph Mireya wrote for her grandmother.

Celebration

Most theme studies include a celebration. Rather than concluding a unit of study with a major test or paper, teachers plan an event that allows students to show how much they have learned. Instead of creating a tense atmosphere that accompanies an exam, teachers organize a time for students to share with their classmates and the teacher.

Grace started the final celebration by reading a newspaper article, "To Live and Die Is to Be Remembered" (Landa 1996), in which the author uses a metaphor of a stone dropped in a pool of water creating a ripple as it sinks to show the impact of the death of a loved one on a person's life. Then Grace shared a picture of her grandmother and reflected on her grandmother's life. In this way, she modeled how she wanted students to respond. She also gave the students specific directions. Following the directions, each student placed a stone in a pool of water in a *metate* (stone dish) as they gave the name of the person they were honoring. After each student shared their memorial epitaph, class members repeated in unison the name of the person being honored. Grace explained what happened:

> As each class member followed in turn, an incredible support network bloomed. Kids brought tissues, gave hugs, *listened* to one another and *celebrated* their lives and families . . . It made us humans together and empowered each of us to know our place in the web. Our shared stories held a mirror to our souls and left us bonded.

Through this theme Grace's students learned what becoming a community meant. They clearly understood the main topic and saw its connection to every activity they did. They developed both vocabulary and concepts as they read and wrote on a topic of great personal meaning to them. They worked closely with their classmates as they studied this universal topic, the death of a loved one.

LA 8 American Folkways · El Dia de los Muertos
(The Day of the Dead)

1. Select a loved one you wish to honor at our "ofrenda"
(table decorated with photographs, poems, stories, flowers.)

2. Write an "epitaph" for this person commemorating
their importance in your life. You may choose:
* poem
* narrative description
* memory of experience

3. Prepare your final draft following this model
and present it to our
class on "El Dia de los
Muertos."

Materials:

· 1 Color "frame" 6"×18"
· 2 White pages 5½"×7"
· 1 Photo or Drawing
· Ink Pen (final draft)
· Colored Markers to
design frame
· Scissors

4. Your piece will be
placed on our
Memorial Wall
after the presentations.

Extra: Design a "calacas" scene,
a shadow box with a clay skeleton
of the deceased engaged in favorite activity.

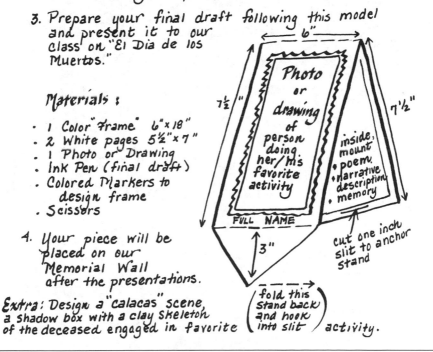

FIGURE 6–5.   *Epitaph Writing Guidelines*

Dear Grandmother
Come in! How glad I am!
I looked for you before,
Put down your hat —
You must have walked-
How out of breath you are!
Dear Grandmother, how
are you? And the rest?
Did you leave Nature well?
Oh, Grandmother come
right upstairs with me,
I have so much to tell!
Did I'd did not get to
say. I am sorry I could
not tell you how much
I love you on the
last of your day's

FIGURE 6–6. *Mireya's Epitaph Writing*

Conclusion

Older English learners represent a real challenge to schools. Both long-term English learners and students with limited formal schooling are far behind their classmates. They have not developed high levels of literacy or many of the academic concepts most students their age have attained. The numbers of these students continue to grow. What are teachers to do?

We realize there are no easy answers to this question. However, there is a growing research base as to what constitutes effective instruction for these students. Researchers are in agreement about the kind of curriculum older English learners need. Based on current research, we have developed four keys to help older English learners close the achievement gap (Figure 1–2).

Translating theory into practice is never easy. For that reason, we have offered many examples from teachers who are succeeding with limited-formal-schooling students and long-term English learners. Sandra, Oscar, and Grace are meeting the challenge. They teach language through content organized around themes that are based on big questions. They connect curriculum to their students' lives. They establish regular routines and use a variety of strategies to scaffold their instruction. Their teaching is consistent with the four keys for school success. We hope their examples will inform and encourage you as you carry out the important work of educating all your students.

Professional Extensions

1. Consider how the strategies that Grace uses fit the four keys to school success. Review Grace's strategies and consider how they might be adapted to the students you work with and the content you teach. Pick out one strategy Grace used, adapt it for your teaching, and use it with your students. Write up the results, including a description of how you adapted the strategy.
2. It is critical to draw on students' first languages and cultures when teaching them. How have you done this in the past, or how will you do this in teaching English learners in the future? List five specific things you have done or plan to do.
3. A key concept we discussed in this book is the importance of developing academic language for older English learners. What are some words and concepts in your subject area that English learners need to understand and be able to use? List them and consider how you might help students acquire them.
4. Review this entire book by looking over chapter titles and main headings. Make a list of the key concepts that have interested you, such as the types of English learners, immigrant and involuntary minorities, or

academic and conversational language proficiency. Make a separate list of the key research about older English learners that has relevance to your teaching. Finally, list strategies that have been described that you might like to try. Share your lists with a receptive and interested colleague.

References

Literature References

Ada, A. F. 1991. *Días y días de poesía*. Carmel, CA: Hampton-Brown.

———. 1992. *Caballito blanco y otras poesías favoritas*. Carmel, CA: Hampton-Brown.

———. 1993. *My Name Is María Isabel*. New York: Atheneum Books.

———. 1997. *Gathering the Sun*. New York: Lothrop, Lee & Shepard.

Ada, A. F., V. J. Harris, and L. B. Hopkins. 1993. *A Chorus of Cultures: Developing Literacy Through Multicultural Poetry*. Carmel, CA: Hampton-Brown.

Atkin, S. B. 1993. *Voices from the Fields: Children of Migrant Farmworkers Tell Their Stories*. Boston: Little, Brown.

Brimmer, L. D. 1992. *A Migrant Family*. Minneapolis: Lerner Publications.

Buirski, N. 1994. *Earth Angels*. San Francisco: Pomegranate Artbooks.

Bunting, E. 1988. *How Many Days to America?* Boston: Clarion Books.

———. 1996. *Going Home*. New York: HarperCollins.

Carden, M., and M. Cappellini. 1997. *I Am of Two Places*. Crystal Lake, IL: Rigby. Also published in Spanish as *Soy de dos lugares*.

Carlson, L., ed. 1994. *Cool Salsa: Bilingual Poems on Growing Up Latino in the United States*. New York: Henry Holt.

Carmichael, E., and C. Sayer. 1997. *The Skeleton at the Feast: The Day of the Dead in Mexico*. Austin: University of Texas Press.

Cisneros, S. 1984. *The House on Mango Street*. New York: Vintage Press.

Climo, S. 1989. *The Egyptian Cinderella*. New York: HarperCollins.

———. 1993. *The Korean Cinderella*. New York: HarperCollins.

———. 1999. *The Persian Cinderella*. New York: HarperCollins.

Coburn, J. R. 1996. *Jouanah: A Hmong Cinderella*. Fremont, CA: Shen's Books.

———. 2000. *Domitila: A Cinderella Tale from the Mexican Tradition*. Fremont, CA: Shen's Books.

Delgado, A. 1994. "Día de los Muertos." In *Cool Salsa: Bilingual Poems on Growing Up Latino in the United States*, edited by L. Carlson. New York: Henry Holt.

Diaz, J. A. 1993. *Pablo Remembers: The Fiesta of the Day of the Dead*. New York: Lothrop, Lee & Shepard.

Drew, D. 1987a. *Animal Clues*. Crystal Lake, IL: Rigby.

———. 1987b. *Caterpillar Diary*. Crystal Lake, IL: Rigby.

———. 1987c. *Mystery Monsters*. Crystal Lake, IL: Rigby.

———. 1988a. *Postcards from the Planets*. Crystal Lake, IL: Rigby.

———. 1988b. *Somewhere in the Universe*. Crystal Lake, IL: Rigby.

———. 1989. *The Life of a Butterfly*. Crystal Lake, IL: Rigby.

Duran, R. 1994. "Border Towns." In *Here Is My Kingdom: Hispanic-American Literature and Art for Young People*, edited by C. Sullivan. New York: Harry Abrams.

Fleischman, P. 1998. *Whirligig*. New York: Dell Laurel Leaf.

Flint, D. 1998. *Where Does Breakfast Come From?* Crystal Lake, IL: Rigby.

Garza, C. L. 1990. *Family Pictures: Cuadros de familia*. San Francisco: Children's Book Press.

———. 1996. *In My Family: En mi familia*. San Francisco: Children's Book Press.

Gilson, J. 1966. *Hello, My Name Is Scrambled Eggs*. New York: Pocket Books.

González, R. 1993. "I Am Joaquin." In *Tapestry: A Multicultural Anthology*, edited by A. Purves. Paramus, NJ: Globe Books.

González-Jensen, M. 1997. *Judge for a Day*. Crystal Lake, IL: Rigby. Also published in Spanish as *Juez por un día*.

Hampton-Brown. 1997. *Into English*. Carmel, CA: Hampton-Brown.

Hickox, R. 1998. *The Golden Sandal*. New York: Holiday House.

Huck, C. 1989. *Princess Furball*. New York: Greenwillow Books.

Jiménez, F. 1997. *The Circuit: Stories from the Life of a Migrant Child*. Albuquerque: University of New Mexico Press.

Johnston, T. 1998. *Bigfoot Cinderrrrella*. New York: G. P. Putnam's Sons.

Keane, S. M. 1997. *Dear Abuelita*. Crystal Lake, IL: Rigby. Also published in Spanish as *Querida abuelita*.

Knight, M. 1993. *Who Belongs Here? An American Story*. Gardiner, ME: Tilbury House.

Mora, P. 2000. *My Own True Name: New and Selected Poems for Young Adults*. Houston: Piñata Books/Arte Publico Press.

Munsch, R. 1980. *The Paperbag Princess*. Toronto, ON: Annick Press. Also published in Spanish as *La princesa vestida con una bolsa de papel* (1990).

Myers, W. 1993. "History of My People." In *Soul Looks Back in Wonder*, edited by T. Feelings. New York: Dial Books.

Nguyen, A. O., and P. Abello. 1997. *Our Trip to Freedom*. Crystal Lake, IL: Rigby. Also published in Spanish as *Nuestro viaje hacia la libertad*.

Okantah, M. 1993. "Windown Morning." In *Soul Looks Back in Wonder*, edited by T. Feelings. New York: Dial Books.

Paulsen, G. 1995. *The Tortilla Factory*. New York: Harcourt Brace. Also published in Spanish as *La Tortillería*.

Pelzer, D. 1995. *A Child Called "It."* Deerfield Beach, FL: Health Communications Incorporated.

Perlman, J. 1992. *Cinderella Penguin, or, the Little Glass Flipper*. New York: Scholastic.

Polacco, P. 1988. *The Keeping Quilt*. New York: Simon and Schuster Books for Young Children.

———. 1990. *Thundercake*. New York: Putnam & Grosset Group.

Rigby. 1997. *Saludos/Greetings* series. Crystal Lake, IL: Rigby.

Rigby. 2000/2001. Theme Packs for English Language Learners. Crystal Lake, IL: Rigby.

Rylant, C., and E. Walker. 1993. "Shoes." In *Something Permanent*. New York: Harcourt Brace.

Say, A. 1993. *Grandfather's Journey*. Boston: Houghton Mifflin. Also published in Spanish as *La jornada de abuelo* (1997).

Sayer, C. 1993. *Mexico: The Day of the Dead*. Boston: Shambhala/Redstone Editions.

Shakur, T. 1999. *The Rose That Grew from Concrete*. New York: Simon and Schuster.

Shroeder, A. 1994. *Lilly and the Wooden Bowl*. New York: Bantam Doubleday Dell Publishing.

Soto, G. 1992. *Living up the Street*. New York: Dell Publications.

———. 1993. *Too Many Tamales*. Carmel, CA: Hampton-Brown.

Steinbeck, J. 1967. *The Grapes of Wrath*. New York: Penguin Books.

Stevens, J., and S. Curmmel. 1999. *Cook-a-Doodle-Doo*. New York: Harcourt, Brace.

Stoodt, J. 1997. *The Biggest Sandwich Ever*. Austin, TX: Steck-Vaughn.

Tatler, S. 1993. *Cookies*. Glenview, IL: Scott Foresman.

Tenorio-Coscarelli, J. 1996. *The Tortilla Quilt*. Murrieta, CA: Quarter Inch.

Thompson, G. 1997. *The Apple Pie Family*. Austin, TX: Steck-Vaughn.

Professional References

1998. Qualities of Effective Programs for Immigrant Adolescents with Limited Schooling. ERIC Digest, July. Report No. EDO-FL-98-07. Washington, DC: Center for Applied Linguistics.

2001. Language Minority Groups in the U.S. National Clearinghouse for Bilingual Education. </www.ncbe.gwu.edu/pathways/demographic/slide2.htm>.

Akmajian, A., R. Demers, and R. Harnish. 1984. *Linguistics: An Introduction to Language and Communication*. Cambridge: MIT Press.

Allington, R., S. Guice, K. Baker, N. Michaelson, and S. Li. 1995. "Access to Books: Variations in Schools and Classrooms." *The Language and Literacy Spectrum* 5: 23–35.

Atwell, N. 1998. *In the Middle: New Understandings About Writing, Reading, and Learning*. Portsmouth, NH: Heinemann.

Barone, M. 2001. "The Many Faces of America. " *U.S. News and World Report* (March 19): 18–20.

Berger, L. R. R. 1996. "Reader Response Journals: You Make the Meaning . . . and How." *Journal of Adolescent and Adult Literacy* 39 (5): 380–85.

Berman, P. 1992. *The Status of Bilingual Education in California*. Berkeley, CA: Paul Berman and Associates.

Brown, H., and B. Cambourne. 1987. *Read and Retell*. Portsmouth, NH: Heinemann.

Bruner, J. 1985. "Models of the Learner." *Educational Researcher* 14 (6): 5–8.

Canedy, D. 2001. "Often Conflicted, Hispanic Girls Drop Out at High Rate." *The Fresno Bee*, 25 March, A 3.

Carrasquillo, A. L., and V. Rodríguez. 1996. *Language Minority Students in the Mainstream Classroom*. Philadephia: Multilingual Matters.

Chang, J. M. 2001. "Monitoring Effective Teaching and Creating a Responsive Learning Environment for Students in Need of Support: A Checklist." *NABE News* 24 (3): 17–18.

Collier, V. 1989. "How Long? A Synthesis of Research on Academic Achievement in a Second Language." *TESOL Quarterly* 23 (3): 509–32.

———. 1992. "A Synthesis of Studies Examining Long-Term Language-Minority Student Data on Academic Achievement." *Bilingual Research Journal* 16 (1 & 2): 187–212.

———. 1995. "Acquiring a Second Language for School." *Directions in Language and Education* 1 (4).

Cooper, D. 1999. *Soar to Success*. Boston: Houghton Mifflin.

Corson, D. 1995. *Using English Words*. New York: Kluwer.

Cortés, C. 1986. "The Education of Language Minority Students: A Contextual Interaction Model." In *Beyond Language: Social and Cultural Factors in Schooling Language Minority Students*, edited by D. Holt, 3–33. Evaluation, Dissemination, and Assessment Center, California State University, Los Angeles.

Cummins, J. 1981. "The Role of Primary Language Development in Promoting Educational Success for Language Minority Students." In *Schooling and Language Minority Students: A Theoretical Framework*, 3–49. Evaluation, Dissemination, and Assessment Center, California State University, Los Angeles.

———. 2000. *Language, Power, and Pedagogy: Bilingual Children in the Crossfire*. Tonawanda, NY: Multilingual Matters.

Darling-Hammond, L., J. Ancess, and B. Falk. 1995. "Collaborative Learning and Assessment at International High School." In *Authentic Assessment in Action: Studies of Schools and Students at Work*. New York: Teachers College Press.

Elley, W. 1991. "Acquiring Literacy in a Second Language: The Effect of Book-Based Programs." *Language Learning* 41 (2): 403–39.

———. 1998. *Raising Literacy Levels in Third World Countries: A Method That Works*. Culver City, CA: Language Education Associates.

Elley, W., and D. Foster. 1996. *Sri Lanka Books in Schools Pilot Project: Final Report*. London: International Book Development.

Elley, W., and F. Mangubhai. 1983. "The Impact of Reading on Second Language Learning." *Reading Research Quarterly* 19: 53–67.

Feitelson, D., and Z. Goldstein. 1986. "Patterns of Book Ownership and Reading to Young Children in Israeli School-Oriented and Nonschool-Oriented Families." *Reading Teacher* 39: 924–30.

Ferris, D., and J. Hedgcock. 1998. *Teaching ESL Composition: Purpose, Process, and Practice*. Mahwah, NJ: Lawrence Erlbaum Associates.

Fleischman, H. L., and P. J. Hopstock. 1993. *Descriptive Study of Services of Limited English Proficient Students*. Vol. 1: *Summary of Findings and Conclusions*. Arlington, VA: Development Associates.

Freeman, A. 2000. Selection of Culturally Relevant Text. Unpublished paper.

Freeman, D. E., and Y. S. Freeman. 2000. *Teaching Reading in Multilingual Classrooms*. Portsmouth, NH: Heinemann.

———. 2001. *Between Worlds: Access to Second Language Acquisition*. 2d ed. Portsmouth, NH: Heinemann.

Freeman, Y. S., and D. E. Freeman. 1996. *Teaching Reading and Writing in Spanish in the Bilingual Classroom*. Portsmouth, NH: Heinemann.

———. 1998a. *ESL/EFL Teaching: Principles for Success*. Portsmouth, NH: Heinemann.

———. 1998b. *La enseñanza de la lectura y la escritura en español en el aula bilingüe*. Portsmouth, NH: Heinemann.

Freeman, Y. S., S. Mercuri, and D. E. Freeman. 2001. "Keys to Success for Bilingual Students with Limited Schooling." *The Bilingual Research Journal* 25 (1, 2): 269–75.

Freire, P., and D. Macedo. 1987. *Literacy: Reading the Word and the World*. South Hadley, MA: Bergin and Garvey.

García, E. 1991. *Characteristics of Effective Teachers for Language Minority Students*. Santa Cruz: National Center for Research on Cultural Diversity and Second-Language Learning, University of California, Santa Cruz.

———. 1999. *Student Cultural Diversity: Understanding and Meeting the Challenge*. Boston: Houghton Mifflin.

García, G. 2000. Lessons from Research: What Is the Length of Time It Takes Limited English Proficient Students to Acquire English and Succeed in an All-English Classroom? Washington, DC: National Clearinghouse for Bilingual Education. <*www.ncbe.gwu.edu/ncbepubs/issuebriefs/ib5.htm*>.

García, O. 1999. "Educating Latino High School Students with Little Formal Schooling." In *So Much to Say: Adolescents, Bilingualism, and ESL in the Secondary School*, edited by C. J. Faltis and P. Wolfe. New York: Teachers College Press.

Gardner, H. 1983. *Frames of Mind*. New York: Basic Books.

George Washington University Center for Excellence. 1996. *Promoting Excellence: Ensuring Academic Services for Limited Proficient Students*. Arlington, VA: Evaluation Assistance Center East.

Gersten, R., and R. T. Jiménez. 1994. "A Delicate Balance: Enhancing Literature Instruction for Students of English as a Second Language." *The Reading Teacher* 47 (6): 438–49.

Goldenberg, C. 1991. *Instructional Conversations and Their Classroom Application*. Los Angeles: National Center for Research on Cultural Diversity and Second Language Learning.

———. 1992. "Instructional Conversations: Promoting Comprehension Through Discussions." *The Reading Teacher* 46 (4): 316–26.

———. 1996. "The Education of Language-Minority Students: Where Are We, and Where Do We Need to Go?" *The Elementary School Journal* 96 (3): 353–61.

Goodman, Y., D. Watson, and C. Burke. 1996. *Reading Strategies: Focus on Comprehension*. Katonah, NY: Richard C. Owen.

Graves, D. 1994. *A Fresh Look at Writing*. Portsmouth, NH: Heinemann.

Hamayan, E. V. 1994. "Language Development of Low-Literacy Students." In *Educating Second Language Children: The Whole Child, the Whole Curriculum, the Whole Community*, edited by F. Genesee. New York: Cambridge University Press.

Hughes, C. A. 2000. Helping Latino Immigrant Students Overcome the Margins: What Schools Can Do to Help. Doctoral dissertation, University of Colorado, Boulder.

Jiménez, R. 2001. "'It's a Difference That Changes Us': An Alternative View of the Language and Literacy Learning Needs of Latina/o Students." *The Reading Teacher* 54 (8): 736–42.

Kagan, S. 1986. "Cooperative Learning and Sociocultural Factors in Schooling." In *Beyond Language: Social and Cultural Factors in Schooling Language Minority Students*, 231–98. Los Angeles: Evaluation, Dissemination, and Assessment Center, California State University.

———. 1988. *Cooperative Learning: Resources for Teachers*. Riverside: University of California, Riverside.

Keene, E., and S. Zimmermann. 1997. *Mosaic of Thought: Teaching Comprehension in a Reader's Workshop*. Portsmouth, NH: Heinemann.

Krashen, S. D. 1982. *Principles and Practice in Second Language Acquisition*. New York: Pergamon Press.

———. 1999. *Three Arguments Against Whole Language and Why They Are Wrong*. Portsmouth, NH: Heinemann.

Krashen, S. D., and T. Terrell. 1983. *The Natural Approach: Language Acquisition in the Classroom*. Hayward, CA: Alemany Press.

Kupetz, M., ed. 1997. *ESL Standards for Pre-K–12 Students*. Alexandria, VA: Teachers of English to Speakers of Other Languages.

Landa, V. 1996. "To Live and Die Is to Be Remembered." *San Antonio Express News*, 3 November, 7.

Lucas, T. 1996. Promoting Secondary School Transitions for Immigrant Adolescents. ERIC Report EDO-FL-97-04. Washington, DC: Center for Applied Linguistics.

———. 1997. *Into, Through, and Beyond Secondary School: Critical Transitions for Immigrant Youths*. McHenry, IL: Center for Applied Linguistics.

Mace-Matluck, B., R. Alexander-Kasparik, and R. Queen. 1998. *Through the Golden Door: Education Approaches to Immigrant Adolescents with Limited Schooling*. McHenry, IL: Delta Systems.

Marsh, L. 1995. "A Spanish Dual Literacy Program: Teaching to the Whole Student." *The Bilingual Research Journal* 19 (3 & 4): 409–28.

McQuillan, J. 1998. *The Literacy Crisis: False Claims, Real Solutions*. Portsmouth, NH: Heinemann.

Mercuri, S. 2000. "Supporting Preliterate Older Emergent Readers to Become Bilingual and Biliterate." *Talking Points* 12 (1): 8–13.

———. 2001. "Tips for Working with Older Students with Limited Formal Schooling." *Bilingual Basics* 4 (1): 6–7.

Moll, L. 1988. "Some Key Issues in Teaching Latino Students." *Language Arts* 65 (5): 465–71.

———. 1994. "Literacy Research in Homes and Classrooms: A Sociocultural Approach." In *Theoretical Models and Processes of Reading*, edited by R. B. Ruddell, M. R. Ruddell, and H. Singer. Newark, DE: International Reading Association.

Moran, C., J. V. Tinajero, J. Stobbe, and I. Tinajero. 1993. "Strategies for Working with Over-age Students." In *The Power of Two Languages*, edited by J. V. Tinajero and A. F. Ada. New York: Macmillan/McGraw Hill School Publishing.

Ogbu, J. 1991. "Immigrant and Involuntary Minorities in Comparative Perspective." In *Minority Status and Schooling: A Comparative Study of Immigrant and Involuntary Minorities*, edited by M. Gibson and J. Ogbu. New York: Garland Publishing.

Olsen, L., and A. Jaramillo. 1999. *Turning the Tides of Exclusion: A Guide for Educators and Advocates for Immigrant Students*. Oakland, CA: California Tomorrow.

Osterling, J. P. 1998. *Moving Beyond Invisibility: The Sociocultural Strengths of the Lation Community (The Case of Arlington's Salvadoran Families)*. San Francisco: American Educational Research Association.

Padrón, Y. N., H. Waxman, A. Brown, and R. Powers. 2000. *Improving Classroom Instruction and Student Learning for Resilient and Non-resilient English Language Learners*. Santa Cruz, CA: Center for Research on Education, Diversity, and Excellence, University of California.

Paiewonsky, E. 1997. "Summary of Statewide Preliminary Pilot Survey on Programs for Over-Age Limited English Proficient Students with Interrupted Formal Schooling." *Idiom* 27 (3): 1, 16.

Palinscar, A. S. 1986. "The Role of Dialogue in Providing Scaffolded Instruction." *Educational Psychologist* 21: 73–98.

Peregoy, S. F., and O. F. Boyle. 2001. *Reading, Writing, and Learning in ESL*. New York: Longman.

Pierce, L., and J. M. O'Malley. 1992. *Performance and Portfolio Assessment for Language Minority Students*. Washington, DC: National Clearinghouse for Bilingual Education.

Purcell-Gates, V. 1995. *Other People's Words: The Cycle of Low Literacy*. Cambridge: Harvard University Press.

Ramírez, J. D. 1991. Final Report: Longitudinal Study of Structured English Immersion Strategy, Early-exit and Late-exit Bilingual Education Programs, U.S. Department of Education. Report #300-87-0156.

Ramos, F., and S. D. Krashen. 1998. "The Impact of One Trip to the Public Library: Making Books Available May Be the Best Incentive for Reading." *The Reading Teacher* 51 (7): 614–15.

Raz, I., and P. Bryant. 1990. "Social Background, Phonological Awareness, and Children's Reading." *British Journal of Developmental Psychology* 8: 209–25.

Rodríguez, T. A. 2001. "From the Known to the Unknown: Using Cognates to Teach English to Spanish-Speaking Literates." *The Reading Teacher* 54 (8): 744–46.

Saunders, W., G. O'Brien, D. Lennon, and J. McLean. 1999. *Successful Transition into Mainstream English: Effective Strategies for Studying Literature.* Santa Cruz, CA: Center for Research on Education, Diversity, and Excellence, University of California, Santa Cruz.

Schifini, A. 1997. "Reading Instruction for the Pre-literate and Struggling Older Student." *Scholastic Literacy Research Paper* 3 (13).

Schumann, J. 1978. *The Pidginization Process: A Model for Second Language Acquisition.* Rowley, MA: Newbury House.

Seufert, P. 1998. Q &A—Refugees as English Language Learners: Issues and Concerns, Center for Applied Linguistics. <*www.cal.org/ncie/DIGESTS/Refugee.htm*>.

Short, D. 1997. *Newcomers: Language and Academic Programs for Recent Immigrants: A Research Summary.* Washington, DC: Center for Applied Linguistics.

Short, K., J. Harste, and C. Burke. 1996. *Creating Classrooms for Authors and Inquirers.* Portsmouth, NH: Heinemann.

Showers, V., B. Joyce, M. Scanlon, and C. Schnaubelt. 1998. "A Second Chance to Learn to Read." *Educational Leadership* 55 (6): 27–30.

Skutnabb-Kangas, T. 1979. *Language in the Process of Cultural Assimilation and Structural Incorporation of Linguistic Minorities.* Washington, DC: National Clearinghouse for Bilingual Education.

Smith, C., B. Constantino, and S. D. Krashen. 1996. "Differences in Print Environment for Children in Beverly Hills, Compton, and Watts." *Emergency Librarian* 24 (4): 8–9.

Summerfield, J. 1986. "Framing Narratives." In *Only Connect,* edited by T. Newkirk. Upper Montclair, NJ: Boynton/Cook.

Thomas, W., and V. Collier. 1997. *School Effectiveness for Language Minority Students.* Washington, DC: National Clearinghouse of Bilingual Education.

Valdés, G. 1996. *Con respeto: Bridging the Distances Between Culturally Diverse Families and Schools.* New York: Teachers College Press.

———. 2001. *Learning and Not Learning English: Latino Students in American Schools.* New York: Teachers College Press.

Vang, T. 2000. Hmong Youth Problems and Its Causes in the United States. Paper presented at fifth annual Interprofessional Collaboration Conference, Fresno, CA.

Von Sprecken, D. 2000. "The Home Run Book: Can One Positive Reading Experience Create a Reader?" *California School Library Association* 23 (2): 8–9.

Vygotsky, L. 1962. *Thought and Language.* Cambridge: MIT Press.

———. 1978. *Mind in Society: The Development of Higher Psychological Processes.* Cambridge: Harvard University Press.

———. 1981. "The Genesis of Higher Mental Functions." In *The Concept of Activity in Soviet Psychology*, edited by J. V. Wertsch. Armonk, NY: M. E. Sharpe.

Walqui, A. 2000. Strategies for Success: Engaging Immigrant Students in Secondary Schools. ERIC Report EDO-FLO-00-03. Washington, DC: Center for Applied Linguistics.

Walsh, C. 1991. "Literacy for School Success: Considerations for Programming and Instruction." In *Literacy Development for Bilingual Students*. Boston: New England Multifunctional Resource Center for Language and Culture Education.

Wang, M. C., G. D. Haertel, et al. 1994. "Educational Resilience in Inner Cities."In *Educational Resilience in Inner-City America: Challenges and Prospects*, edited by M. C. Wang and E. W. Gordon. Hillsdale, NJ: Lawrence Erlbaum.

Weaver, C. 1996. *Teaching Grammar in Context*. Portsmouth, NH: Boynton/Cook.

Williams, J. 2001. "Classroom Conversations: Opportunities to Learn for ESL Students in Mainstream Classrooms." *The Reading Teacher* 54 (8): 750–57.

Winfield, L. F. 1991. "Resilience, Schooling, and Development in African American Youth: A Conceptual Framework." *Education and Urban Society* 24: 5–14.

Wink, J. 1993. "Labels Often Reflect Educators' Beliefs and Practices." *BEOutreach* 4 (2): 28–29.

Worthy, J. 1996. "Removing Barriers to Voluntary Reading for Reluctant Readers: The Role of School and Classroom Libraries." *Language Arts* 73: 483–92.

Yankay, C. 1997. "Planning for the Over-Age Limited English Proficient IFS Student in the World of Work: A School-to-Work Program at Liberty High School, New York City." *Idiom* 27 (3): 4–5.

Index